# The Museum of Contemporary Art: The Panza Collection

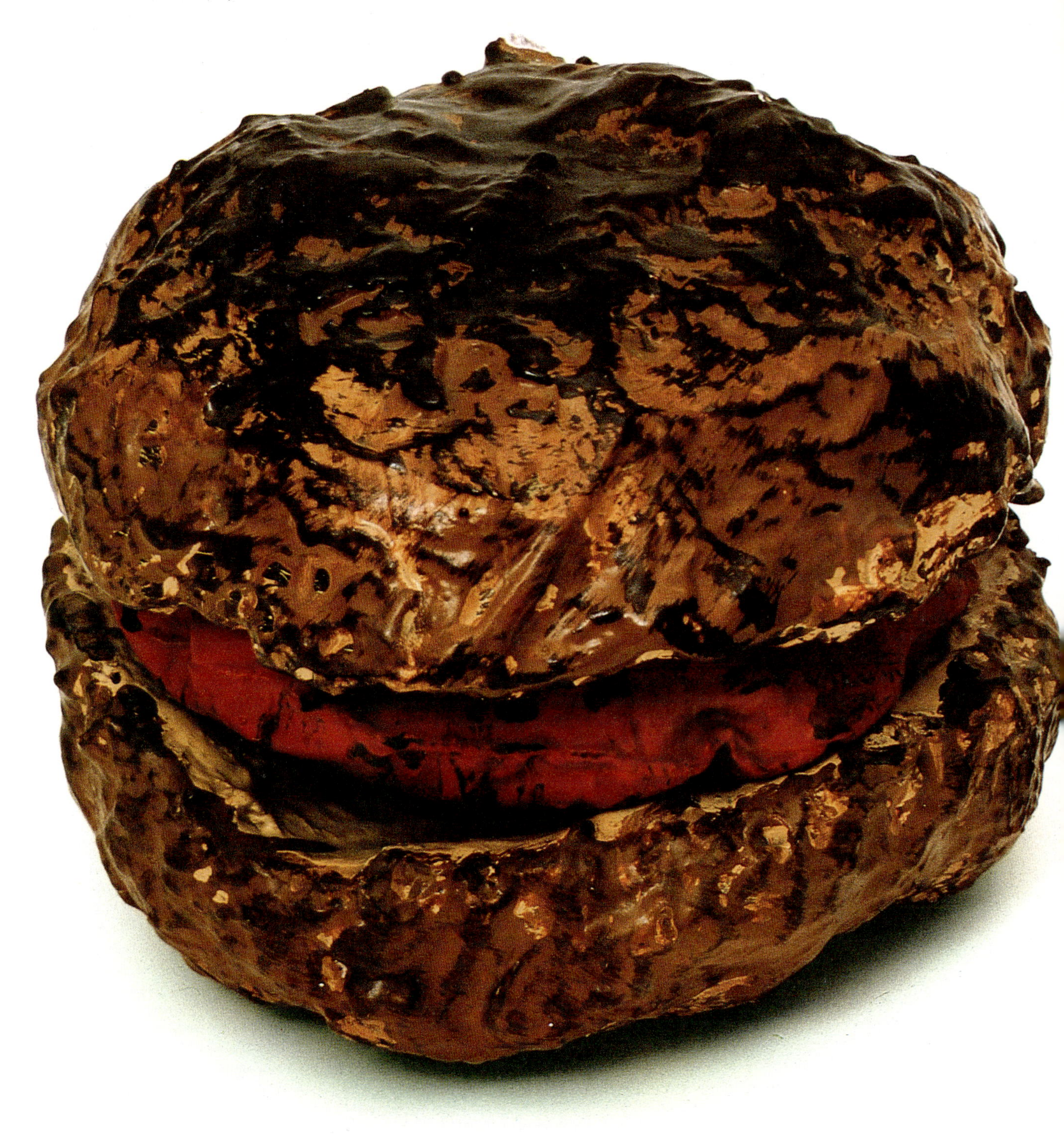

# The Museum of Contemporary Art: The Panza Collection

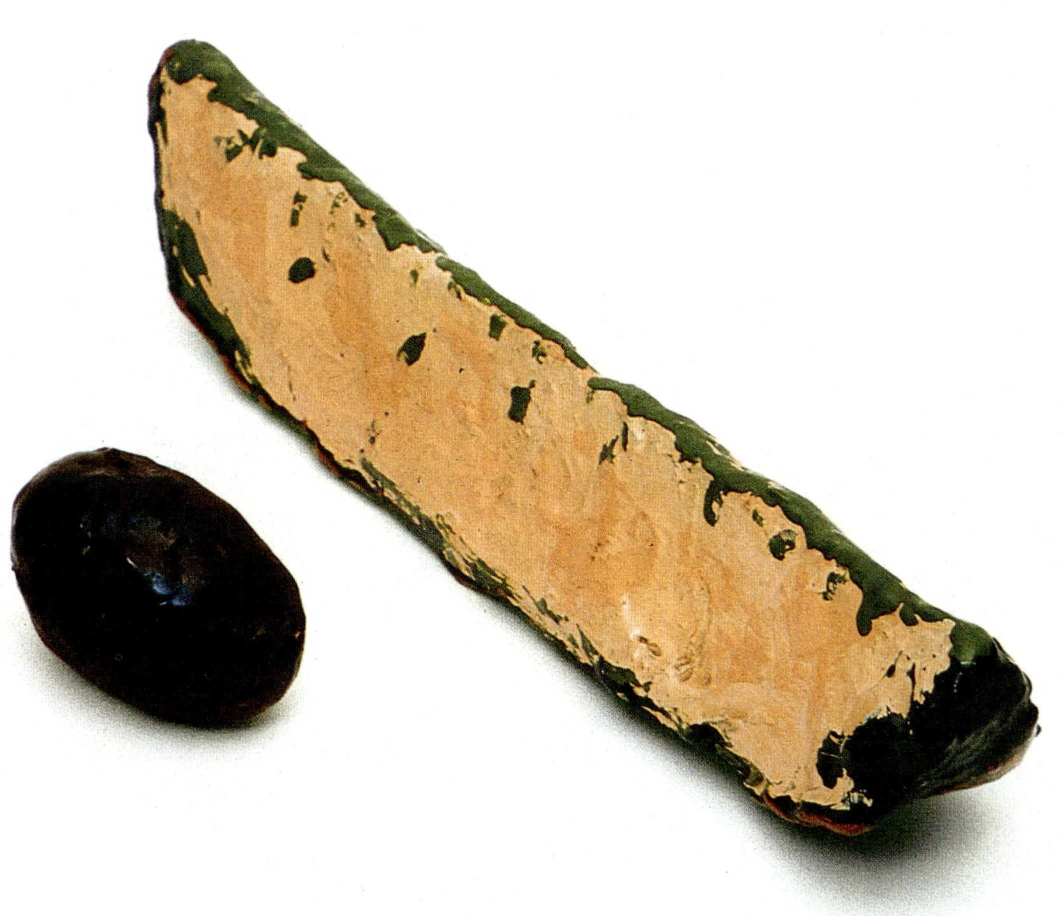

The Museum of Contemporary Art, Los Angeles

This catalogue is published on the occasion of the exhibition
**The Museum of Contemporary Art: The Panza Collection,**
February 13–September 29, 1985.

Editor: Julia Brown

Editorial Assistant: Kerry Brougher



Library of Congress Catalogue Card Number: 84-043083

ISBN: 0-914357-09-3

Design: Massimo Vignelli

Photographs: Gian Sinigaglia and Squidds and Nunns

Printed in Italy by LS Graphics, New York

## Acknowledgments

On behalf of The Museum of Contemporary Art, I would like to express our sincere gratitude to Giuseppe and Giovanna Panza di Biumo of Milan, Italy for their overwhelming kindness and generous cooperation. They have patiently given of their time and energy during all aspects of the organization of this special exhibition. The design of the installation, in the spaces of The Temporary Contemporary, presenting these important works of art in Southern California for the first time, was developed by Dr. Panza.

I gratefully acknowledge the important assistance and advice of members of the Board of Trustees of The Museum of Contemporary Art. Their innovative leadership and commitment to the development of The Museum of Contemporary Art has made possible the acquisition and the exhibition of these major works. Particular thanks are due Founding Chairman Eli Broad who, as the earliest supporter of this acquisition, provided the leadership that led to the agreement between the Museum and Dr. and Mrs. Panza. I appreciate greatly the involvement and support provided by Morton Winston, Chairman, Acquisitions Committee; Lenore S. Greenberg, Chairman, Program Committee; and Betye Monell Burton, Chairman, Community Relations Committee. William F. Kieschnick, Chairman and Frederick Nicholas, Vice Chairman, have provided much appreciated encouragement and assistance. David S. Tappan was responsible for arranging the appropriate funding for the exhibition and catalogue.

I extend thanks to Massimo and Lella Vignelli who provided the elegant graphic design for the exhibition catalogue and installation. Photographic documentation of the works in the exhibition was superbly provided by Gian Sinigaglia and Squidds and Nunns.

Many members of the staff of The Museum of Contemporary Art were actively involved with the acquisition and exhibition: Julia Brown, Senior Curator, was completely responsible as curator and editor, for coordination and development of the exhibition and its catalogue. During the first year in The Temporary Contemporary she has assumed, with care and sensitivity, the responsibility for an extensive series of exhibitions and catalogues, among them *The First Show,* and the work of Michael Heizer, Robert Therrien, Dan Flavin, Mark Lere and Betye Saar. Sherri Geldin, Administrator, provided crucial assistance with the administration related to the Museum overall to realize this project and its exhibition; Kerry Brougher, Assistant Curator, conducted the interview with Dr. Panza published in this catalogue and assisted Julia Brown with all aspects of the organization and preparation of the exhibition and catalogue; Kim Bradley, Registrar, supervised the details of registration and shipment from Zurich, Switzerland to Los Angeles; John Bowsher and his installation assistants worked on the shipment from Zurich, with special assistance by Alitalia and Flying Tigers, and on complicated technical aspects of the exhibition installation at The Temporary Contemporary. Assistant Curator Elizabeth Smith and curatorial interns Connie Butler and Ellen Kwan, assisted in manuscript preparation.

*Richard Koshalek*
*Director*

## Introduction

The great collections of art are more than an accumulation of objects. They are personal in nature, reflecting contact between the maker and the collector, a sharing of ideas transmitted through the work of art. The collection of Giuseppe and Giovanna Panza di Biumo is such a collection. Built with great care and sensitivity over time and chosen when the work was new and untested, the Panza collection of approximately 600 objects spans the periods of 1936 to 1975 and includes from one to sixty examples of work by fifty-nine artists. As a whole the collection reflects a concentration and careful selection of the work of a number of artists, rather than an encyclopedic version of a period. The scope of the Panza collection is in its commitments and depth, reflecting an affinity to the ideas embodied in the work, both in his decision regarding individual works and in the group of works as a whole.

The eighty works gathered here in The Temporary Contemporary in an exhibition installation designed by Dr. Panza, represent the earliest part of his collection and a group of works that have been purchased by The Museum of Contemporary Art, becoming the foundation of the Museum's permanent collection. This is the first time these works have been exhibited together.

These works were collected by Dr. Panza between 1956 and 1963 and comprise a significant statement about American and European art of the mid-forties through the mid-sixties. By collecting the work of nine then-emerging artists in depth, Dr. Panza formed the beginning of his collection of contemporary art. As he did in the rest of his collection he concentrated on a particular period or body of work by each artist as what he felt was the strongest and most pivotal period of that artist's works at the time.

They include work by two Europeans and eight Americans. Six paintings from the "Hostages" and "Naked Torsos" series by French artist Jean Fautrier, dating from the early to mid-forties, evoke the devastation of wartime Europe in their anguished, visceral, anthropomorphic qualities. These works prefigured the nascent "art informel" movement of postwar Europe. The Spanish painter Antoni Tàpies is represented in the collection by fourteen paintings from 1955-59. These years, during which Tàpies realized his style of "matter painting," constitute the period of his greatest influence.

The works of American artists collected by Dr. Panza include twelve paintings in black and white by Franz Kline, dating from 1953-61, with one work in color, *Alva*, from 1958. Seven paintings by Mark Rothko are statements of the artist's mature period between 1953-60 of rich, darkly-hued shapes hovering within fields of color.

The "combines" of the mid-fifties by Robert Rauschenberg are among the best-known works in the collection. Well-known works of assemblage such as *Interview*, *Coca-Cola Plan* and *Factum I* prefigured widespread use of popular and common imagery in the sixties. The sixteen works by Claes Oldenburg were acquired by Dr. Panza from "The Store," an installation of 1961 in a storefront containing sculpture of transformed everyday objects formed from clots of painted plaster.

James Rosenquist's eight works from the early sixties—emblematic, epic views of American objects in unlikely juxtapositions—explore formal issues of scale, selectivity, abstraction, using commercial advertising techniques. Four paintings by Roy Lichtenstein, all from 1962, represent the artist's

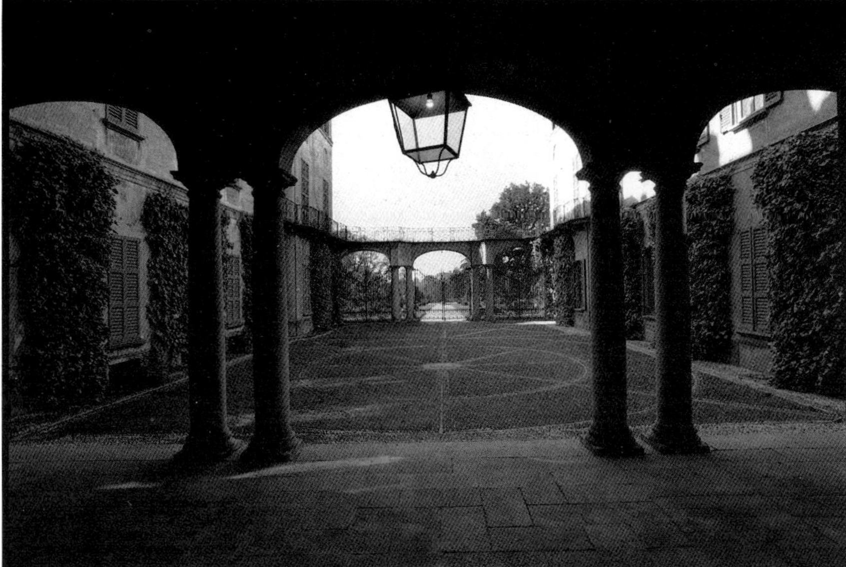

1

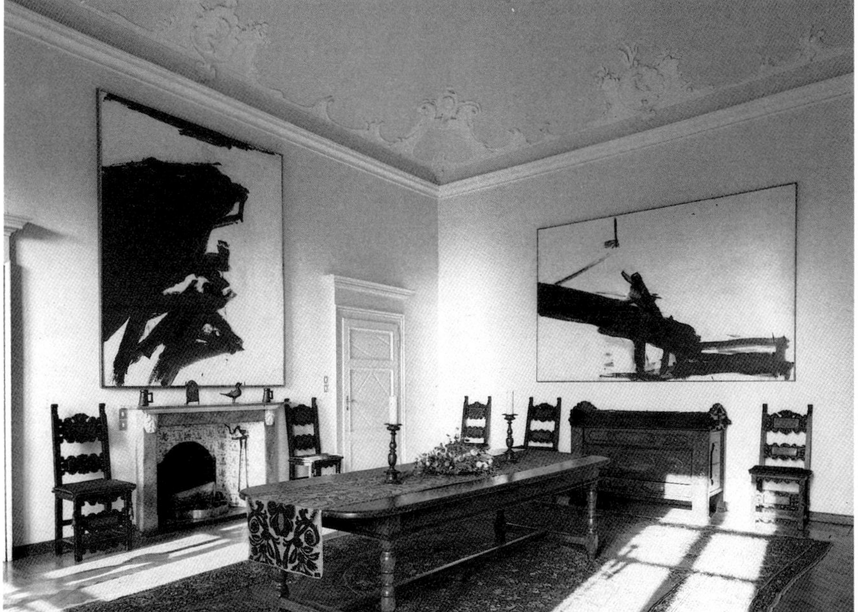

2

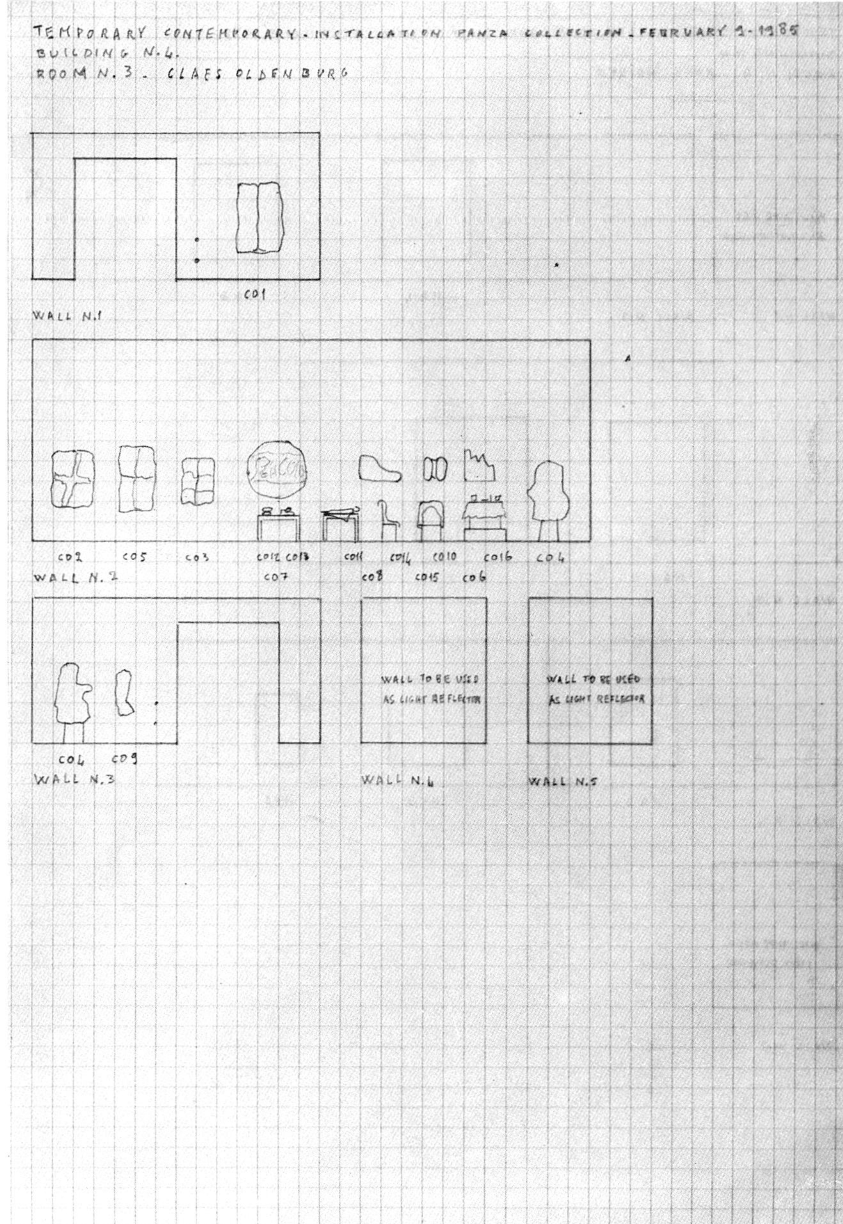


3

*1. Villa Menafoglio Litta Panza, Varese, Italy, c. 1750*

*2. Installation of Franz Kline's* Orleans, *1959, and* Monitor, *1956, Varese*

*3. Giuseppe Panza di Biumo's plan for installation of Claes Oldenburg's work at The Temporary Contemporary*

4

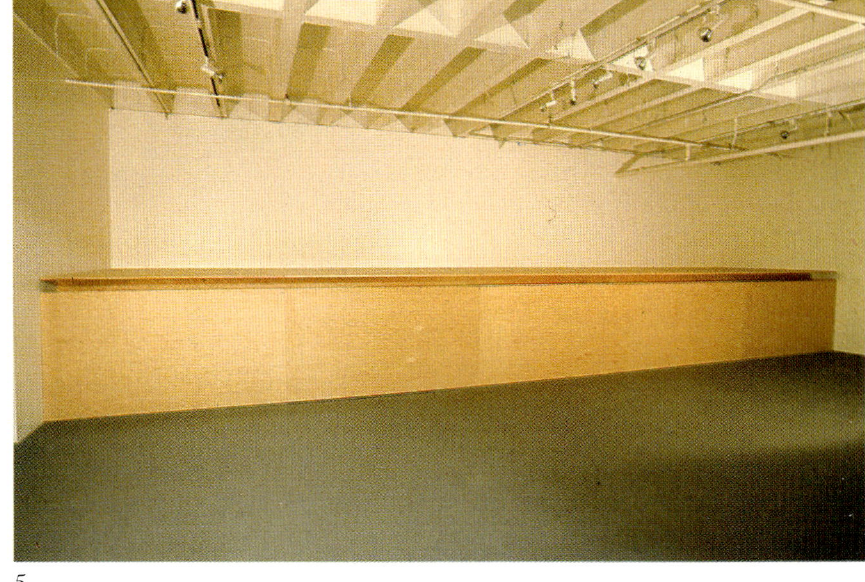

5

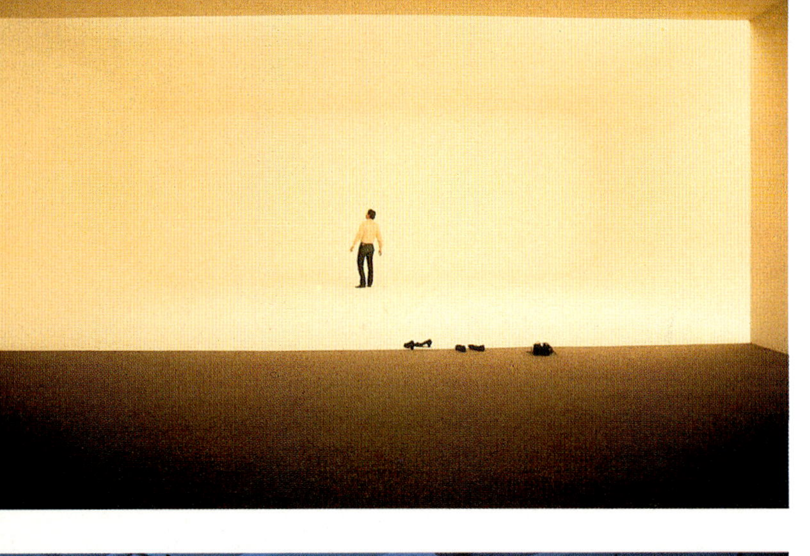

6

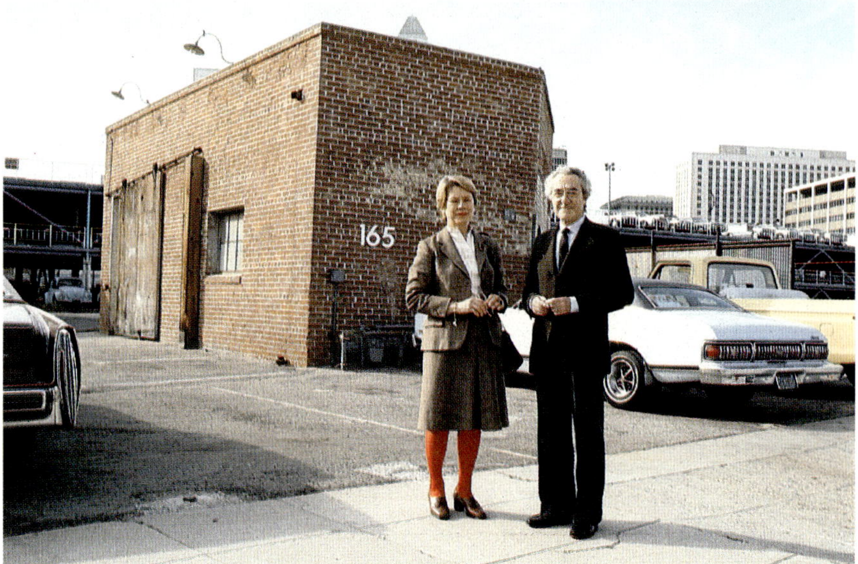


7

*4. Doug Wheeler,*
SA MI DW SM 2 75 TC LA, *1975*
*Installation at The Temporary Contemporary for* The First Show, *1983*
*Collection of Giuseppe and Giovanna Panza di Biumo*

*5. Donald Judd,* Untitled, *1974*
*Plywood, dimensions variable*
*Installation at The Temporary Contemporary for* The First Show, *1983*
*Collection of Giuseppe and Giovanna Panza di Biumo*

*6. Dan Flavin,* Untitled *(to Flavin Starbuck Judd), 1968*
*Blue and red fluorescent light, dimensions variable*
*Installation at The Temporary Contemporary for* The First Show, *1983*
*Collection of Giuseppe and Giovanna Panza di Biumo*

*7. Giuseppe and Giovanna Panza di Biumo in front of the 165 North Central building of The Temporary Contemporary*

stylistic crystallization of bold, linear images culled from mass culture and art history. Two sculptures by George Segal from the mid- to late-sixties, *Man in the Armchair* and *Sunbathers on the Rooftop,* use the human figure to comment on the alienation of contemporary life.

These works were among the first collected by Dr. Panza. In the mid-sixties he collected a major concentration of the work of Donald Judd, Dan Flavin, Bruce Nauman, Sol LeWitt and Richard Serra, among others, and in the early seventies collected works in the form of proposals and plans by artists such as James Turrell, Robert Irwin, Doug Wheeler and Maria Nordman, a number of which have been installed in his villa in Varese and were reconstructed at The Temporary Contemporary for *The First Show: Painting and Sculpture from Eight Collections, 1940-80*.

Dr. Panza has a long-standing interest, involvement and commitment to artists in Southern California. As one of the few individuals to collect and realize the work of environmental artists in Southern California, Dr. Panza has made numerous trips, since the mid-sixties, to Los Angeles to visit studios. In November 1980, with an introduction from artist Robert Irwin, Dr. Panza joined the Board of Trustees of The Museum of Contemporary Art and has continued his commitment to California and its art community through his active participation and support of this institution. In November 1983 selections from the Panza collection comprised one of eight collections for *The First Show,* the opening exhibition of The Museum of Contemporary Art in The Temporary Contemporary. On June 28, 1983 Dr. Panza wrote to the Museum regarding his interest in placing works from his collection in a public institution outside Italy and his concern for finding the appropriate place to house this portion of his collection. This letter led to the purchase by The Museum of Contemporary Art, several months later, of the eighty works gathered together in this catalogue.

The Museum of Contemporary Art, as it plans for its new building on Bunker Hill and the expected long-term use of The Temporary Contemporary, will build its collection on these works and around the concept they embody: the private vision presented in a respectful way for the public and the concentration on the work of individual artists. In turn, the concentration on the individual creator in a larger historical context will be reflected in the exhibition program.

The collection of The Museum of Contemporary Art has also been enriched by works from other private collections such as that of Robert A. Rowan of Pasadena, who has also made in-depth commitments to a number of artists including Frank Stella, Morris Louis, and Jules Olitski as well as having an ongoing involvement with the work of younger California artists. As the first individual to donate works to the permanent collection of the Museum, Robert Rowan had an early belief in the partnership between the individual and the public institution which is carried on here with the Panza collection. This relationship will be continued by other collectors of contemporary art and will be vital to the formation and growth of The Museum of Contemporary Art.

*Richard Koshalek*
*Director*

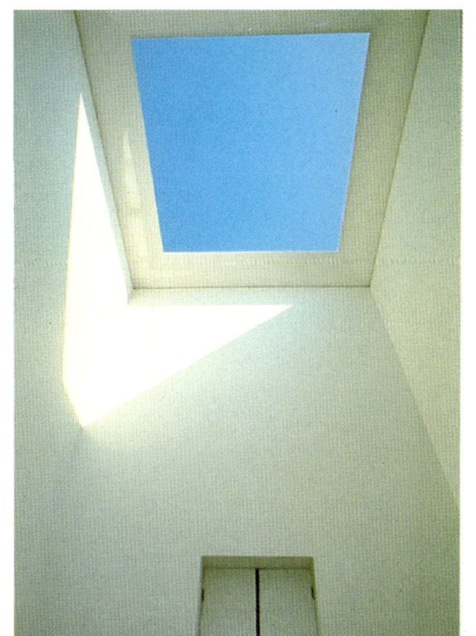

*8*

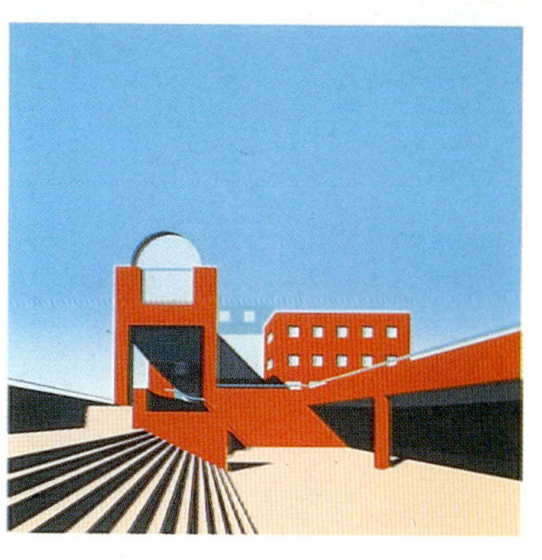

*9*

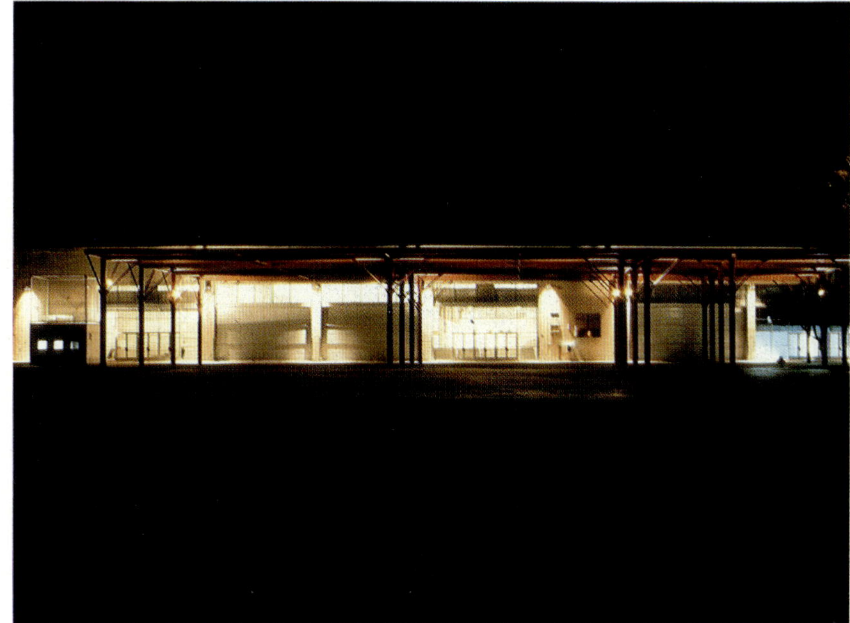

*10*

*8. James Turrell,* Skyspace, *1972*
*Executed at Varese, 1974*
*Collection of Giuseppe and Giovanna Panza di Biumo*

*9 Rendering of The Museum of Contemporary Art, Los Angeles*
*Arata Ioszaki, architect*
*Silkscreen by Arata Isozaki, 1983*

*10. The Temporary Contemporary, Los Angeles*
*Frank Gehry, architect*

**Interview with Dr. Giuseppe Panza di Biumo**
**Kerry Brougher**

*October 25, 1984*
*Los Angeles*

*Kerry Brougher: Why did you collect these works?*
Giuseppe Panza: I felt that this art was very close to my feelings, close to a view I had of a relationship between man and society. These artists wished to overcome limits. This intention is very clear in the work of many Abstract Expressionists; there is a deep feeling of something related to a reality that we try to understand but that we cannot reach, a constant tension between what we have and what we don't have. The thing we don't have is not a tangible thing, not an object, but something beyond human possibilities, something we feel a strong need for. This is a metaphysical attitude; this desire has no limits. It clashes with the reality of life as it is.
I was looking for something close to my judgment about art and life. I always felt the need for art to show what is important in the life of every person. Art is just a way to visualize this expectation.

*KB: How did you arrive at the approach of collecting in depth?*
GP: I have a strong relationship to the works I like. When I have an interest in the personality of the artist, I want to have more of his work. It is my way of being a part of the artist's work. I found a way to make a connection with another person through the work of art. I can have a relationship to somebody else in a deep way through art, because art relates what a man feels and thinks. The work of an artist is the history of his life. Each work is a moment of his life.

*KB: There is something you get from an artist by seeing a group of works together that you might not get from an individual work.*
GP: Yes, we see a different attitude, different parts of a personality; we are not ever in a static situation. Our situation always changes even if it has a common character because our personality and our wishes give direction to our state of mind. But this state of mind changes, and we try to find what it is based on to maintain our state of mind in a given direction.

*KB: Could you talk about these eighty works? Perhaps we could start with Jean Fautrier and Franz Kline.*
GP: Chronologically the first artist whose works I collected was Fautrier. The works I have were made between 1944 and 1947, which I believe was a core period for this artist. Fautrier made expressionist paintings in the twenties but stopped in the thirties. He started to paint again during the second World War, stopped again in '47, and resumed painting after '51. There are big differences between the three periods. The first one is expressionist, the last more colorful, more relaxed. But I believe the first and the last are less interesting than the most important middle period, which included the paintings made during the second World War and the three years after the world war.
These paintings are closely related to the war. They are called *Otage*, which means "hostage." These paintings represent people who were killed by the Germans during the war. The paintings are both abstract and figurative. They represent dead people who are still in some way warm bodies although they have already lost life. This contradiction between death and life and the expression of the ancient dual condition of existence are very powerful. Few artists have been able to express this opposed situation. In order to express life, Fautrier used beautiful color with a French sensibility, the kind of color used by the Impressionists. This was a really sophisticated use of colors. But at the same time, he used dark colors to show the existence of something related to death. He used thick impasto; there is no flat

color left on the canvas. This thick impasto gives a three-dimensional quality to the paintings. Because it's fragmented, it gives a strong feeling of something broken. Life was broken by the violence of the war, and this situation is clearly and strongly expressed in these works, not only in an expressionist way, like that of the German Expressionists during the first World War or before, but in a more sophisticated way, using not just a stronger placement of color but also the relationship of pigments to each other.

*KB: And it's something that could probably only be experienced by a European coming out of the second World War.*
GP: Yes, Fautrier expressed the tragedy of the war.

*KB: Was the next artist whose work you collected Kline or Tàpies?*
GP: Kline *and* Tàpies. Kline began to make abstract art in 1950, Tàpies in '55. Franz Kline interested me because of the strength of his painting, the energy revealed by the sign he made on the canvas, not only with the hand but by moving the arm and the body. The gesture is extremely important. The energy that came from the movement of the whole body of the artist is the opposite of that manifested in painting made by European artists in the twenties and thirties. Traditionally, European painting was generally small in size and executed with small brushes. When the brush is short and the painting small, we feel a focused concentration of expression. In Europe before and during the second World War, the artist was just one person outside a situation which was contrary to his morals. The only way to be safe was to be alone with the small canvas, and it did not make sense to make it bigger.
But Kline was the opposite. Along with the other Abstract Expressionist artists from America, Kline's attitude changed, because these artists felt the need to be active in a real situation, not to remain within an intellectual space that was individual and ineffective. They needed to be present in a situation that other people shared because they had the will and the energy to express the inner human condition in a broad way and to have relationships with others. Because of this, Jackson Pollock made his drip paintings, and Franz Kline used the gesture in his own big way. I believe Pollock and Kline are the most American artists of this period, both had this kind of strong energy.
The experience of these paintings is like looking at the city of New York when we arrive from Europe; it is a completely different situation. We see a vertical city and have a great feeling, just an eruption of energy going up to the sky. We don't know where this energy will lead. The goal is unclear because the sky is something without limit. But this energy is also an unlimited human energy. This human strength that we feel in New York is something very powerful, and Kline's constructions in black and white represent this situation.

*KB: Could you talk a little bit about the differences between Kline and Mark Rothko?*
GP: Yes. Kline expressed this energy. Rothko is a man who looked inside himself. He expressed not the real need to make art but the need to be and to think about the inner condition. What is great in Rothko is his vision of a capacity of man to discover and handle the world inside his own mind. At the same time we have a relationship to the experience of being in New York. When you see a sunset in Manhattan, you see the colors in Rothko's paintings. When you see the sunset between two skyscrapers, you have a Rothko, because the huge rectangular shape catches a part of the sky. Rothko's color gives you the notion of color that is real and not real at the same time because it's endless. It is not only a surface but a space that doesn't have an end. When you look at the color of Rothko, you feel the space is endless, just as when you look inside yourself, you feel your experience of life is something endless. Rothko's work has no boundaries.

*KB: Could you tell us about Tàpies?*
GP: Tàpies is a Spanish artist related to the Spanish tradition and psychological situation of El Greco but also closely related to what happened in Europe after the second World War. The war was a very traumatic experience, because what was essential in Western civilization was broken. What happened in Europe had never happened before in history in such a tragic way. In some way the second World War was the end of Europe. Politically after 1945, Europe was no longer the center of the world. Before, the power and reach of Europe had been endless; it had control of all the continents, had discovered and colonized America, and had control of China and India. After 1945 everything disappeared, because power changed hands. This also was the end of substantial moral values because millions of people were killed, not killed in war, but killed through a plan intended to destroy people. The work of Tàpies expressed the conflicting situation of Europe after this traumatic experience. The values that came from the Renaissance, the values of cultivated man, had changed, because during the war rational values were used for killing people. The art of Tàpies shows how this situation destroyed the beliefs of the European people.

*KB: I'd like to continue to talk about some of the other artists whose work you collected at this time, such as Robert Rauschenberg.*
GP: Rauschenberg is very interesting in an opposite way from Rothko. Rothko's work is the exploration of the feeling hiding in each person, which is extremely rich because the mind of a man is the greatest thing that exists in nature. But Rauschenberg explores other aspects of human beings that are extremely important, such as memory. Memory distinguishes human beings because without memory we would be like insects that cannot avoid the planned scheme. But man has freedom because of memory. Only through memory can he have options, have judgments about what is good and what is not good for his goals. This is possible because we have a memory. This exploration is extremely important because it gives us the possibility of recreating what no longer exists. This capacity to create the past is great because the past is rich in bad and good things. Through memory we can actualize what was good in our past and enjoy the present.
This process takes place through observing objects. Everything we have used belongs to a part of our life because we have lived with it. These objects are in some way related to what happens to your body, to your life, because you have lived with them. Rauschenberg has a great capacity to establish this relationship between our past and the object that is a witness to our past. When we look at this work, it is like reading a book; we see the history of a person. Each image has a relationship to some recognizable event, which contains a memory through which we can become adults.
The events most strongly impressed in our memory happen when we are young. This is a great power, to make present what was so important, so beautiful in the distant past, in the faraway events of your life when you were very young. Rauschenberg uses objects as images to make this relationship.

This is a process that was begun by Marcel Duchamp. Duchamp showed how found objects could become a means of communication with all past experience. He was able to make his own shapes out of the function of a useful object. He made powerful objects that made analogies. We are able to establish a relationship between different objects because of their common qualities. We are intelligent because we are able to establish a relationship between different objects and events. The process of thinking is to make a judgment from individual experience and to make a relationship between different experiences that embody a common idea. This is a process that Duchamp made possible with the common found object. Before Duchamp it was necessary to use common images in order to make a relationship to an idea. But Duchamp discovered that it was not necessary to use real images; rather, you could use something that had a relationship to the image, to the event, to evoke another event in your mind.

This was something that was also understood by Leonardo da Vinci. When you look at a painting by Leonardo da Vinci, you see something, but when you look at it a second time, you see something else. If you spent half an hour in front of a Leonardo painting, you would see several different expressions, different meanings, different situations. What was a painting of a single image would become a world that was rich in many different relationships. Duchamp discovered that this process could be applied to one object, because the capacity of man to think is unlimited.

*KB: So Rauschenberg's work remains somewhat ambiguous?*

GP: Yes. This was the great thing that Rauschenberg developed from Duchamp and Leonardo.

*KB: Could you discuss the work of the other Pop artists you collected: Claes Oldenburg, Roy Lichtenstein, James Rosenquist, and George Segal?*

GP: Oldenburg did a lot with Rauschenberg's process but in a different way. Rauschenberg's work was related mainly to the past, while the work of Oldenburg was related to objects that are present in your life. We disregard the objects we use everyday because after we use them we are tired of them. But in a way these objects become a part of your life as a witness to what happened. If we pay attention, we can make a history of a man through the objects he uses because those objects are typical of a period. A company makes a particular kind of container to attract attention and to convince the consumer to use a product. We know attention fades away when something lasts too long. The company making the product changes the image of the object in order to renew demand because the image is different. For this reason, objects belong to a given period of our life. If we pay attention, we realize that objects are important as witnesses of history. Instead of making copies of a Greek Venus, it is perhaps more interesting to make copies of a container of Coca-Cola. This container is more important to us than the Venus de Milo, which is an ideal beauty and different from our standard of beauty. Though the Venus is something fine, we are more interested in something more relevant than this ideal realization of a human body. The Coca-Cola can tell us much more about our life than the Venus de Milo. To make a monument out of this common object can be beautiful. Oldenburg used bright colors and made shapes in plaster in close approximation to a Coca-Cola container. They became a monument devoted to our history and to the real history of our everyday life, not the history we read in a book, but an artifact of the life of a person who drinks Coca-Cola.

Lichtenstein follows a similar process to Oldenburg's, but he uses a two-dimensional surface for making images of everyday life. He uses images taken from advertising and comics, the kind of literature we have all around us. It is entertainment or advertisement, an inducement to buy more and to spend money, or entertainment when we are tired or traveling on the bus or subway. It is an entertainment that we evolve from an exterior part of our brain and that doesn't take any kind of strength or energy in order to be understood. It is popular literature that everybody reads and knows. In some ways it is more real to us than Shakespeare or Dante. In order to read Shakespeare and Dante, which is a great experience but also really demanding, our attention has to be concentrated on what we are reading. After one hour of reading, we have to stop because we feel tired. But we can read the comics every day for several hours, and we don't get tired. Surely we are bored, but not tired.

Lichtenstein pursued the possibility that this common factor and connection to life for millions of people could be interesting and that these popular images could have intellectual qualities. In order to achieve this goal, an archetypal model had to be made out of these images. They had to become something beautiful like the Greek Venus and to utilize the same technique: good proportion and harmonic relationships between shapes and color. In this way the real images became an abstraction because it was no longer just the common object that was depicted in painting, but an intellectual transformation of something common. Lichtenstein's work belongs to the classical mode of making paintings, because it used the same kind of relationship between shapes and colors but used popular images rather than images out of a classical tradition. His work is completely different from the realistic paintings of the nineteenth-century, when the goal of a good artist was to deliver a presentation of something that looked real or like something that happened in history. It is not the goal of Lichtenstein to make mythical images.

Rosenquist used the same technique and had a similar aim as Oldenburg and Lichtenstein, but used a different organization of images. He was a sign painter of big billboards and was able to make images very big in order that they could be seen from far away. He had to be able to condense an image of something that every person could recognize and understand in a fraction of a second. It is important that the image be so powerful in order to keep our attention for a short time but at the same time to tell us what we need to know. This is the secret of a good advertisement. Rosenquist understood this process and used it. This is advertising's practical function. But beyond this, we can put together images in a manner that becomes critical of our society—a reason why we make what we make. We can show the contradiction between what we have, which is made popular by advertisements, and what is actually important in our existence. This makes it clear that, in order to be happy, we must reach for something else besides what advertising images say are necessary. Happiness is something more and this metaphysical question of life is shown by the images Rosenquist puts together.

George Segal is related to the other Pop artists, but his work has a direct relationship to the images and expressions of the human body. What is important for Segal is not only the figure but using all parts of the body to represent and gather information about who we are. In order to do this he makes an imprint of the body, even using the suit we wear everyday because we are dressed in a given way, and this is part of what makes our personality and our situation in life. But because this distant photograph of life becomes something that not only exists for one second but becomes fixed and made in a lasting material, it becomes an image of a situation that is in some way permanent. We change, but we are always the same. Time passes, and our body changes, but what happened today is very similar to what happened before. The fact that we are able to have this lasting imprint of the passing time gives a kind of endless existence to something which is really short-lived.

*KB: In your collecting, how did you choose the individual works? Were the artists involved at all in your choices?*

GP: No, the artist was never involved in the specific choice, because very often the artist had his own ideas, which were different from mine. Artists have a special interest in the works they make that is related to the goal they have. Sometimes there were works which were not interesting to me but were interesting to the artist. It was always my choice, though sometimes the artist was influential. Information I gained from dealers and critics was also useful because it made it possible to see more work and have more information in order to make a judgment. But the judgment was mostly mine because when you deal with contemporary art the judgment is always black and white. Some people say the art is good, and the same number of people say it is not good. If you make your choice based on the opinion of others, you make nothing because you have the same number of nos and the same numbers of yeses. You have to choose for yourself.

*KB: How were these works received in Europe at the time you were purchasing them?*

GP: The reaction was very negative. A few people became interested because they felt that this work had a very great strength. But mostly people refused to take it seriously and said of Kline, for example, "This painting was made by splashing black color on the canvas and anyone would be able to do it." That was the general opinion.

There was also opposition because French dealers felt the competition from America. They felt they risked losing control of the market. Until 1956 the art market was still in Paris, and everybody willing to buy art was going to Paris, not New York. They felt I was one of the first to break this reputation of Paris as the center of the art world.

*KB: It's not easy to be the first.*

GP: Well, it was not too difficult because nobody was able to stop what I was doing because I was doing it for myself, and it was not related to ordinary interest.

*KB: Could you explain your particular interest in American art?*

GP: It is very simple. America has had many more great artists in the last thirty years than Europe.

*KB: Why do you think that is?*

GP: By the forties America had reached a cultural maturity. It had become a country that was not only interested in economic development but that possessed a rich culture. This happened because a good educational system was developed. The American people are very well-educated, more so than, for instance, the Italians. This was the best condition in which to start a kind of renaissance, because America had the intellectual capacity to produce great art. Surely European culture was essential in making American culture because of the artists' roots and the influence during the war of influential artists like Fernand Léger, Joan Miró, and André Masson, but at the same time 1945 was the start of an independent culture.

*KB: What do you see as the differences between art in Europe and America in the forties and fifties?*
GP: European artists were more related to history, while American artists felt the need to build something new and essential from nothing. American artists went through a process of finding an essential situation and a way to build a new way of life, a new vision of life. The European artists were more involved with the past, the culture inherited from centuries before. This kind of situation is limited because the past is great, but if you are too much involved with the past, you don't get out of it; you are in the past, you're not in the future. Creation is making the future, not remaking the past; otherwise it is not creation, it is imitation. In order to do something new, we have to be alone in front of reality, without the help of something already completed. For Europeans, the presence of a past culture was an advantage that became a limit. Americans were more bold, ready to risk more. Their will to risk attracted me, their will to risk everything, because for the American artist art was a way of life, not just an intellectual amusement, and it was something extremely important for itself. They were risking a life, not just a painting. This is a great difference.

*KB: You've talked at other times about your concern with installation in regard to the rest of your collection, particularly works by artists such as Robert Irwin, Maria Nordman, Donald Judd, Doug Wheeler, and others. What are your ideas concerning presentation for these earlier works?*

GP: The process is different but not too different because my goal was to have enough work of each artist to make an environment. I believe that only when you are in a room filled with the work of a single artist are you in the right situation to understand their work. Each individual work helps you to understand the work as a whole. If you have work of another artist with a different personality, in some way it stops you, because you have to change your view, your opinion, your state of mind. But when the room is filled with work of the same artist, you are inside the mind of that artist. You are inside an environment because the works around you give you the same energy, they make the same kind of intuitive communication. You feel something out of a painting that isn't tangible but is strong. A kind of magnetic force; strength that is realized by each painting fills the space and fills you.

*KB: How do these eighty works fit into the rest of your collection?*
GP: These works were a starting point for my collection and related to a time of my personal history. Also they are an interpretation of a time in history.

*KB: Could you comment on your thoughts concerning how you would like to see these works presented in the future?*
GP: I hope it will be possible to present them in the way we are doing here, in this exhibition, giving each artist a room in which the works can be seen without other influences that would disturb the attention of the viewer. To make an environment in each room is the ideal situation I wish to have, to have space that gives the viewer a peaceful environment and encourages a process of learning the work without distracting shapes inside the room. It is important to see only what we have to see.

*KB: Could you comment on your interest in Los Angeles and in this part of your collection coming here?*
GP: One of the many reasons I want these paintings here is the fact that many of the artists whose work I have in my collection are from Los Angeles. Their work is the history in some way of what happened in Los Angeles, an interpretation of the life of this city. Because Los Angeles is a new city, it needs art. Cities without art and without museums where art will be chosen and shown to the public in a permanent way are not true cities, because a museum is a measure of the level of quality of the life of a society. Without a museum, we don't have this measure. The more beautiful the museum, the better the life must be inside the city, because people are able to judge what is good and what is less good in life. Art shows a sensibility and capacity to make a distinction between what is good and not good in life.

**The reproductions in the following section are one-tenth the size of the actual works.**

# JEAN FAUTRIER

**Nude,** 1943
*Oil on paper, 21½ x 15 in.*

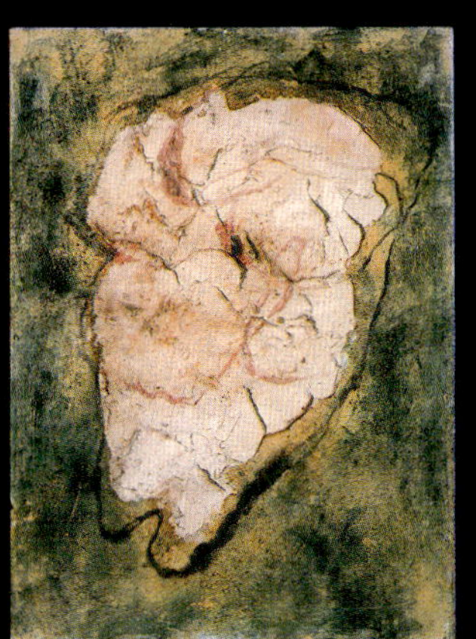

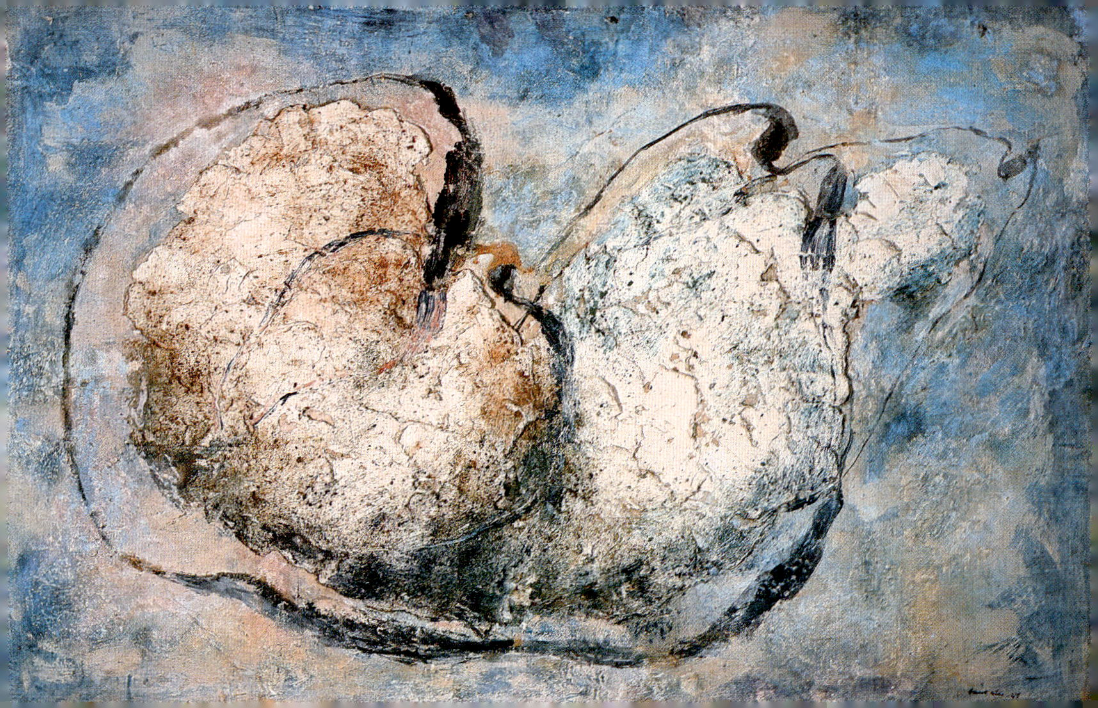

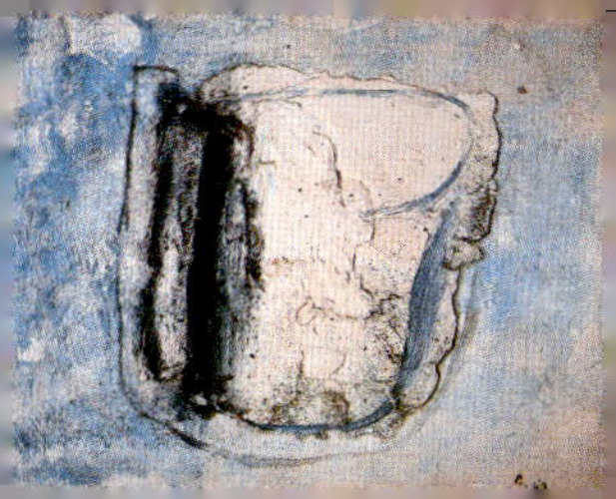

# FRANZ KLINE

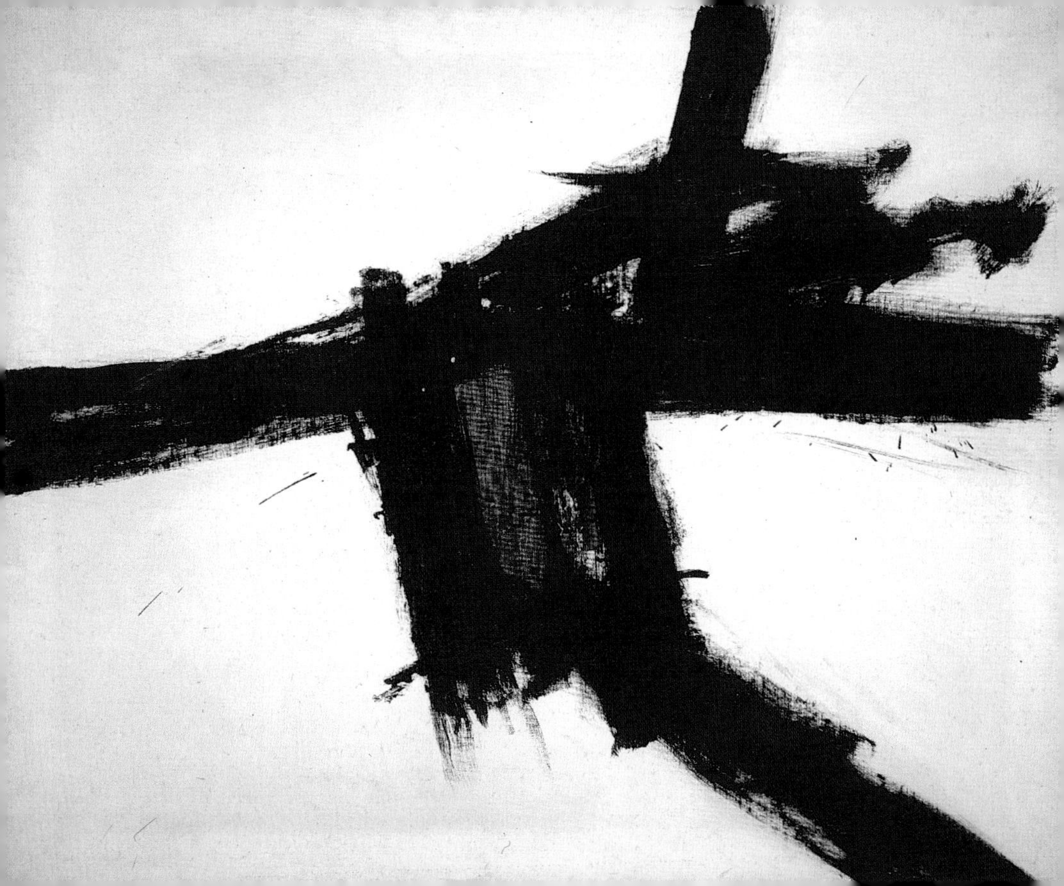

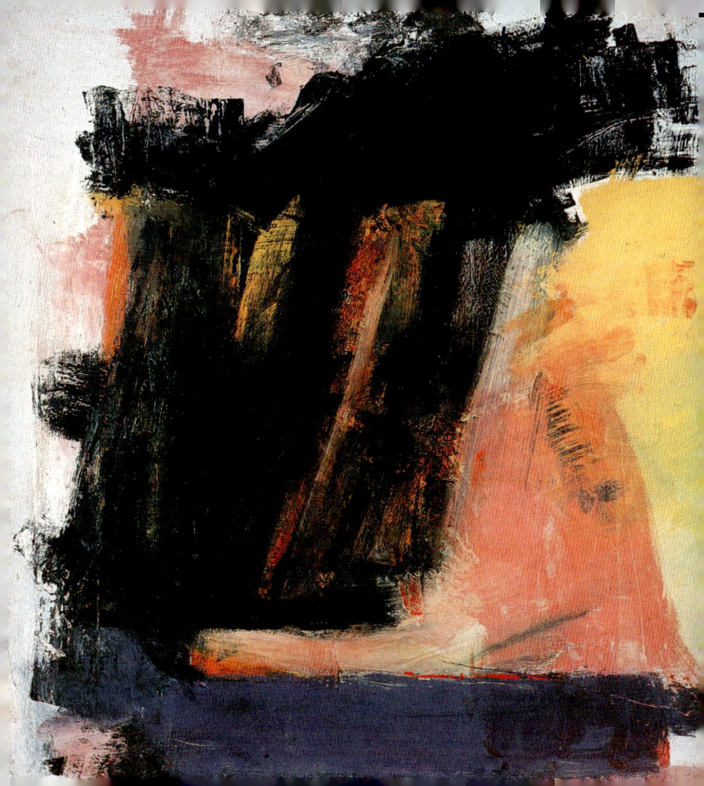

ROY LICHTENSTEIN

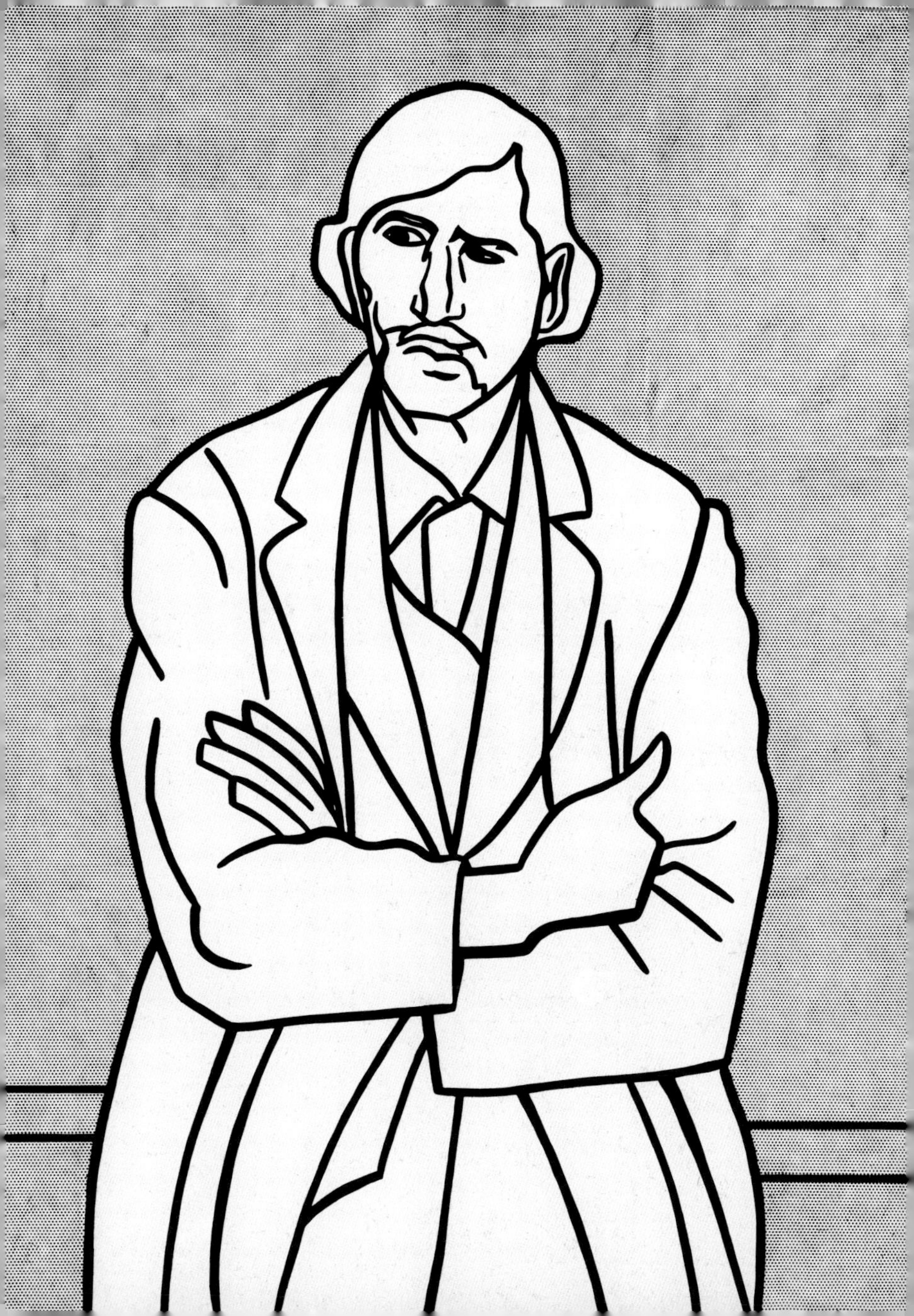

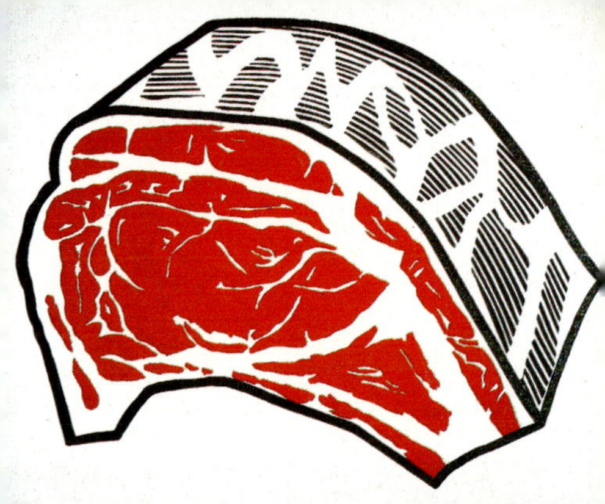

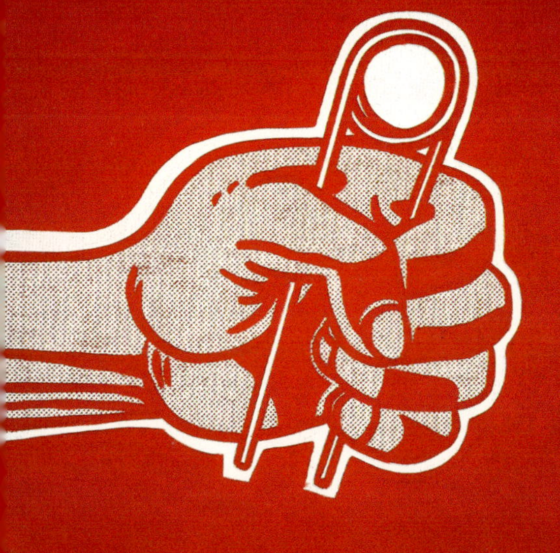

## CLAES OLDENBURG

**Blue and Pink Panties,** 1961
*Plaster-soaked muslin over wire frame, painted with enamel, 62¼ x 34¾ x 6 in.*

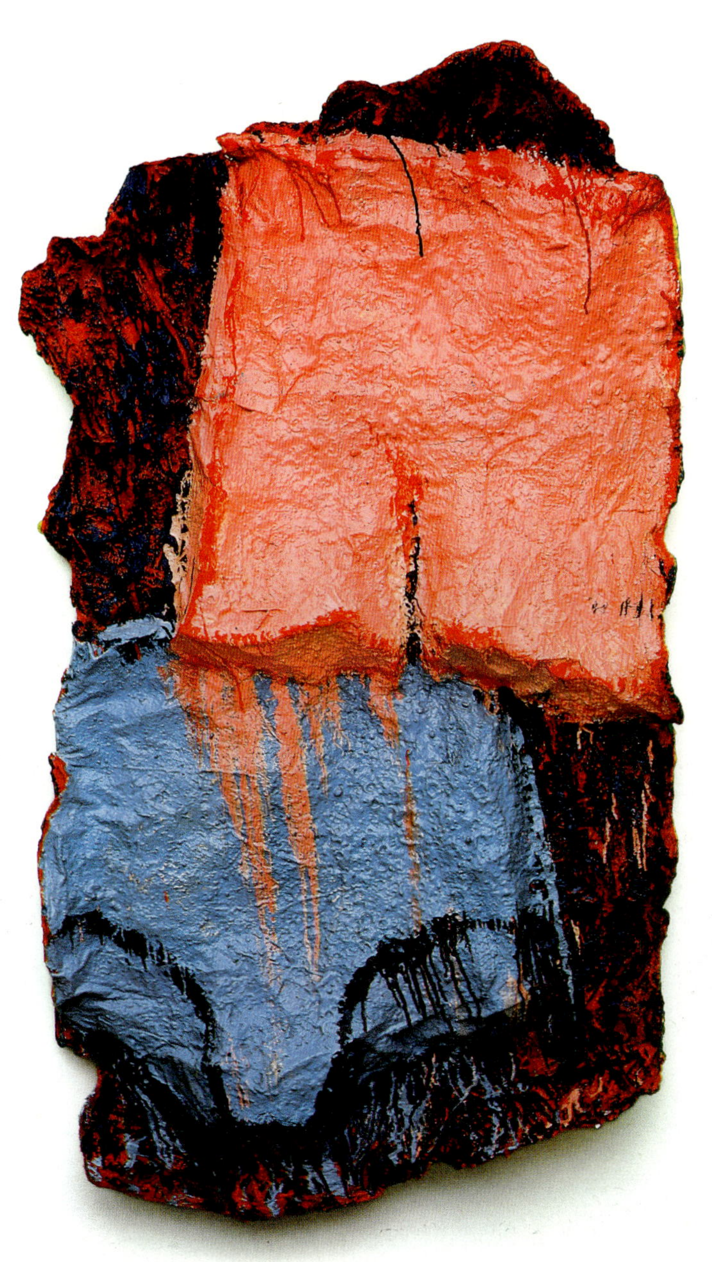

**Pepsi-Cola,** 1961
*Plaster-soaked muslin over wire frame, painted with enamel, 58¼ x 46½ x 7½ in.*

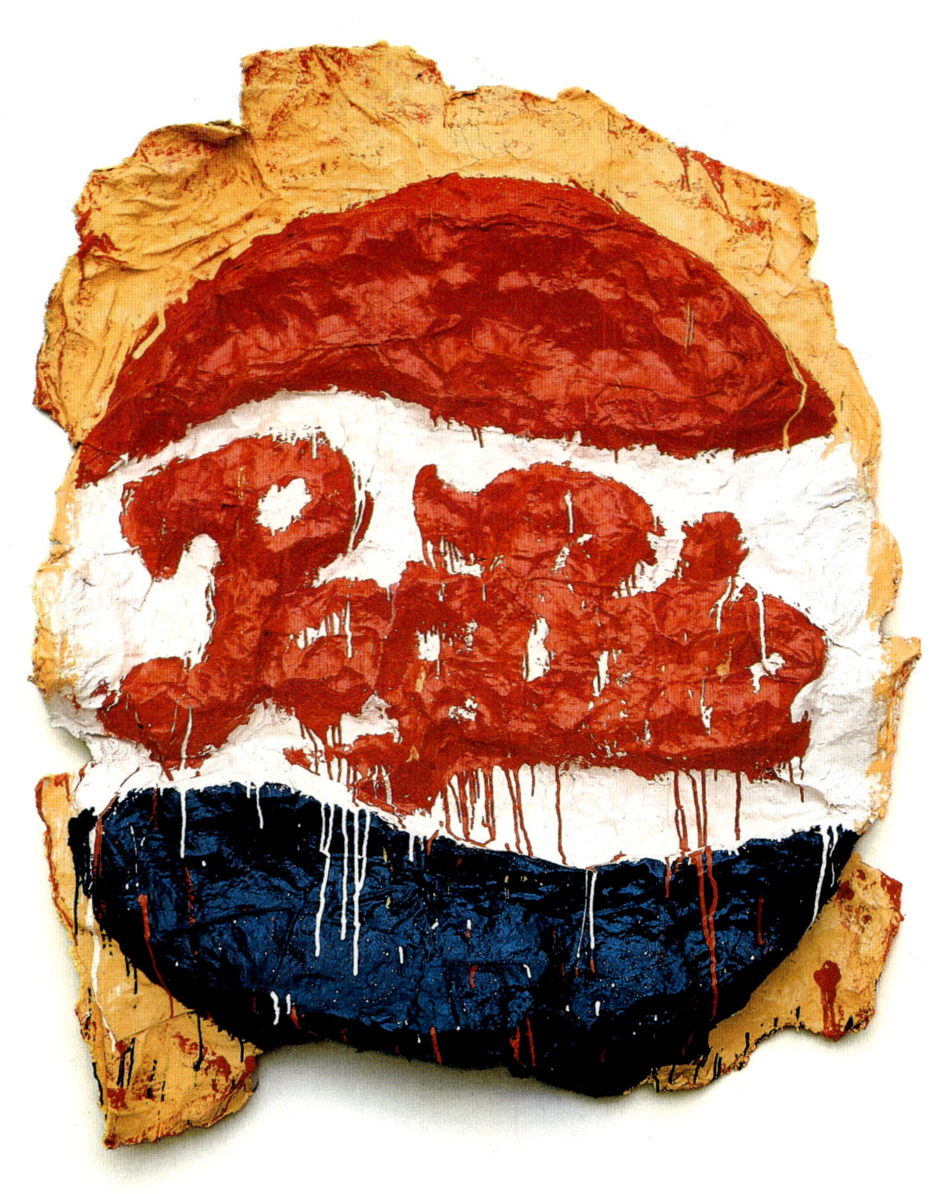

**Blue Pants on Chair,** 1962
*Plaster-soaked muslin over wire frame, painted with enamel, 37 x 17 x 26¾ in.*

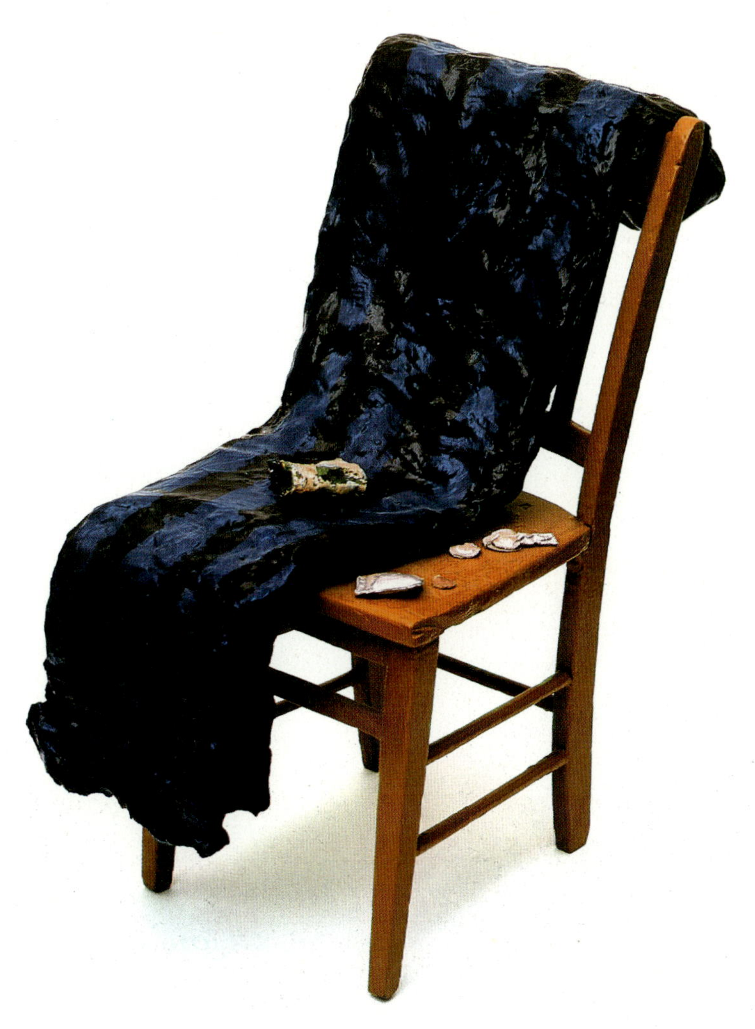

ROBERT RAUSCHENBERG

**Interview, 1955**
*Combine painting, 72¾ x 49¼ in.*

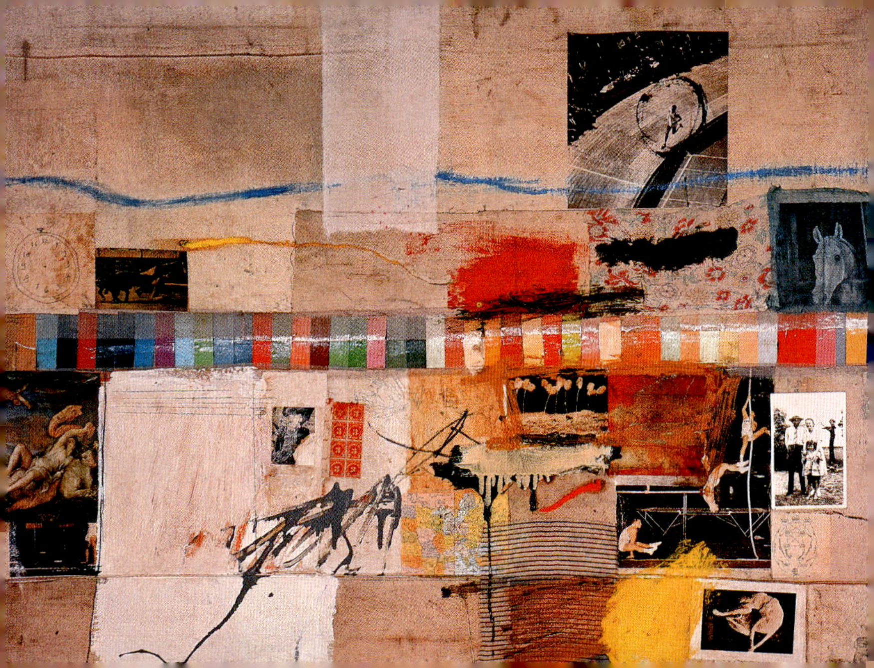

**Coca-Cola Plan,** 1958
*Combine painting,*
*26¾ x 25¼ x 4¾ in.*

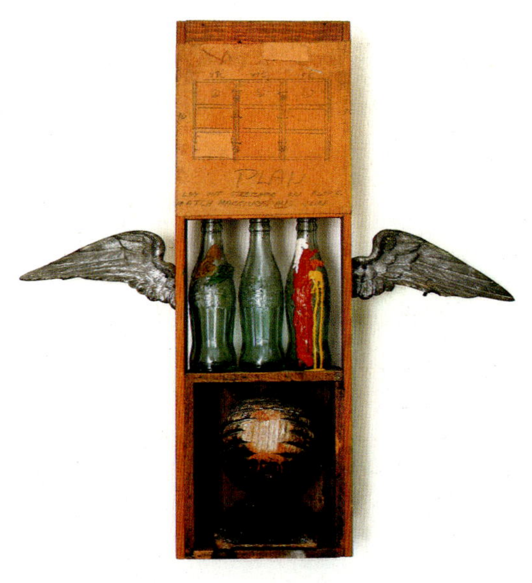

# JAMES ROSENQUIST

**Push Button,** 1960-61
*Oil on canvas, 82¾ x 105½ in.*

**Vestigal Appendage,** 1962
*Oil on canvas, 72 x 93¼ in.*

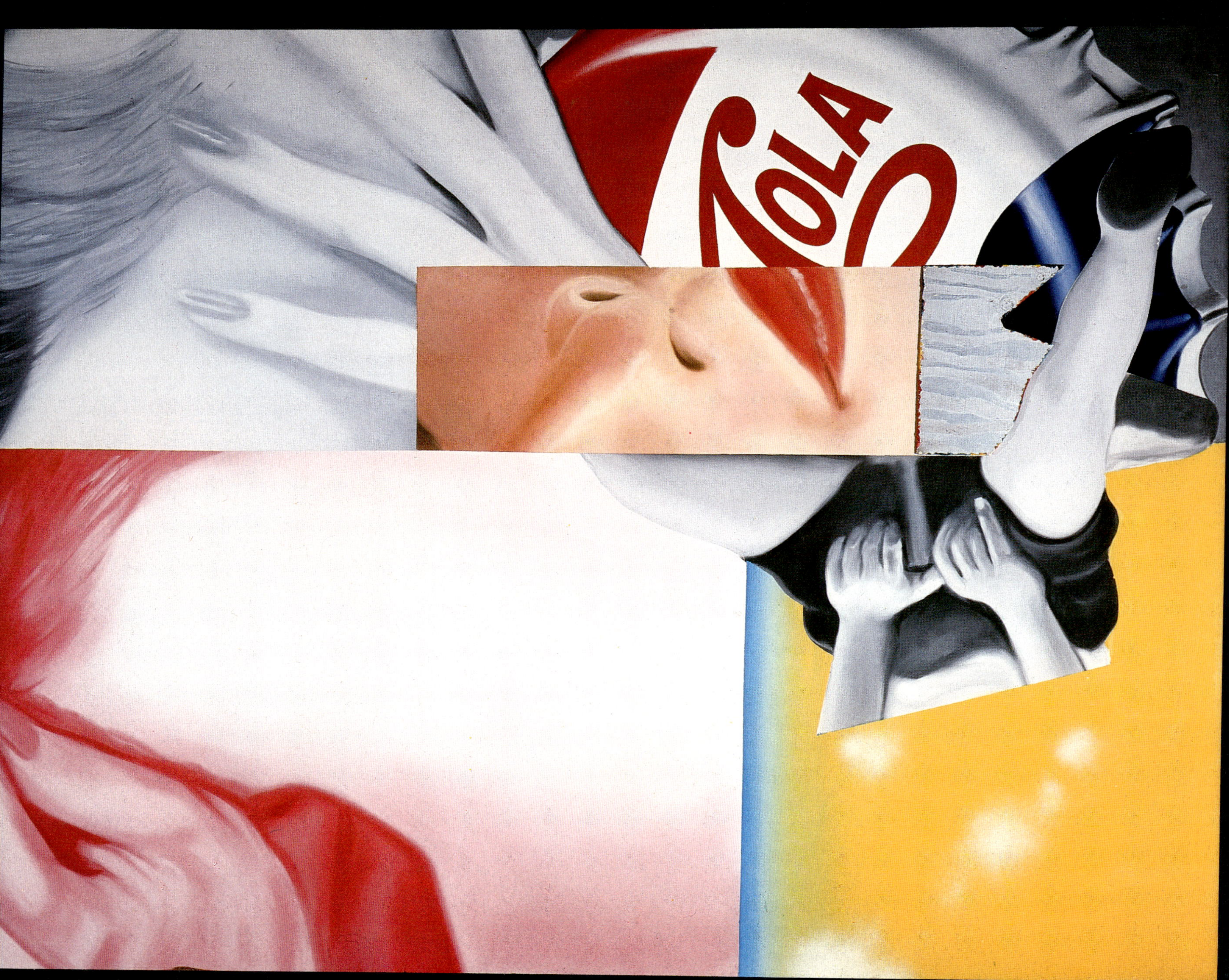

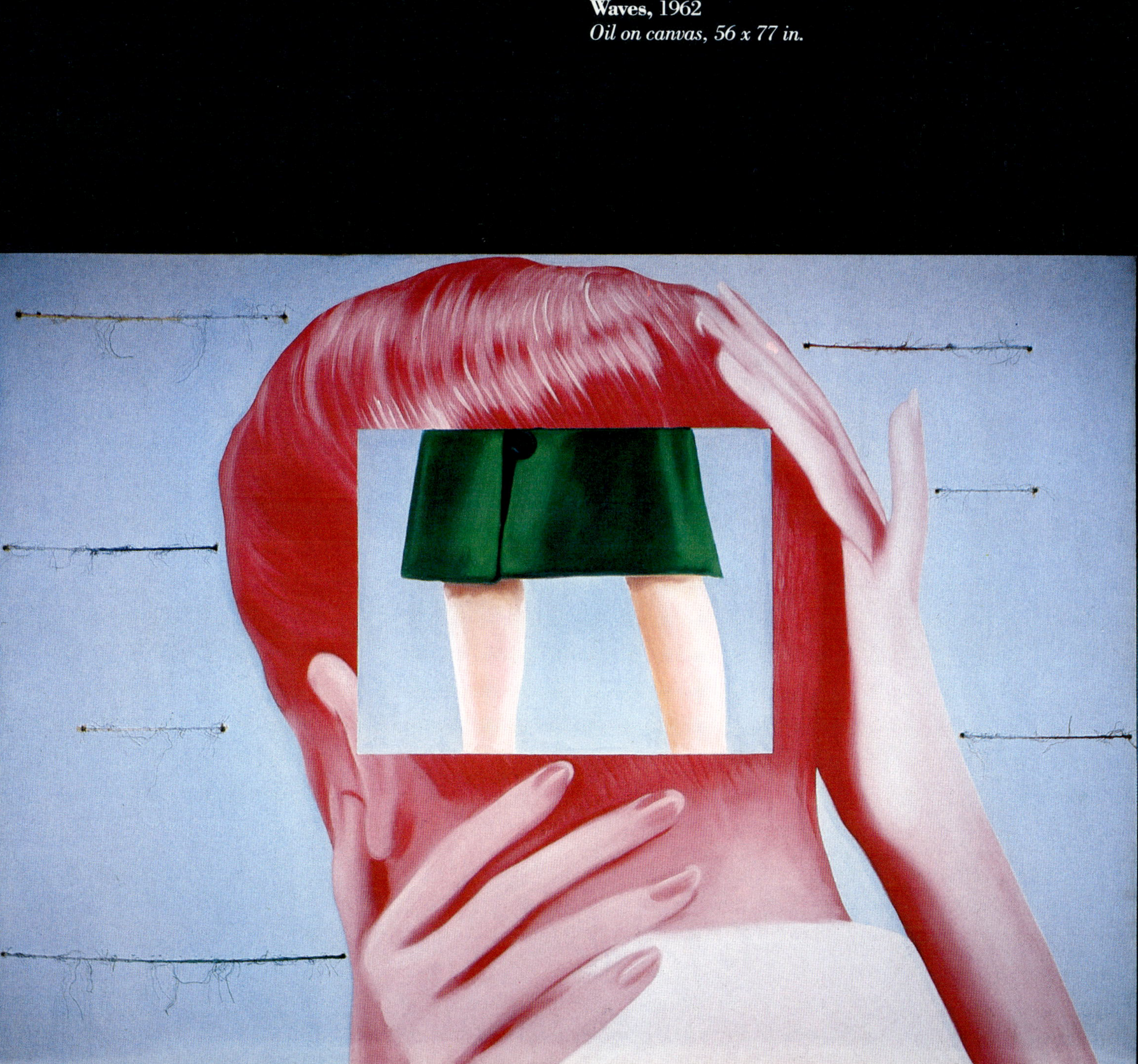

**Waves,** 1962
*Oil on canvas, 56 x 77 in.*

**Violet and Yellow on Rose,**
1954
*Oil on canvas, 83½ x 67¾ in.*

# MARK ROTHKO

# GEORGE SEGAL

**Man in the Armchair,** 1969
*Plaster and wood,*
*49½ x 30 x 31½ in.*

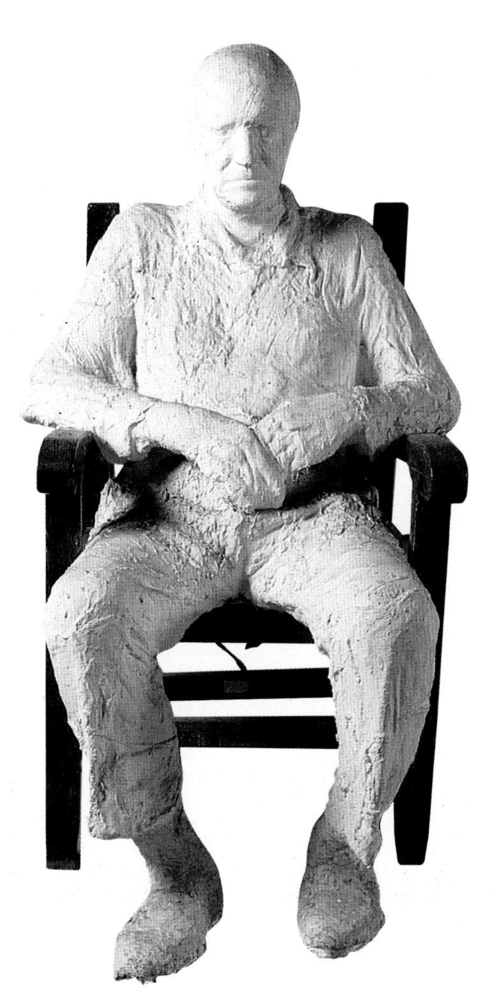

**Sunbathers on Rooftop,**
1963-67
*Plaster and wood,*
*34¼ x 143½ x 96 in.*

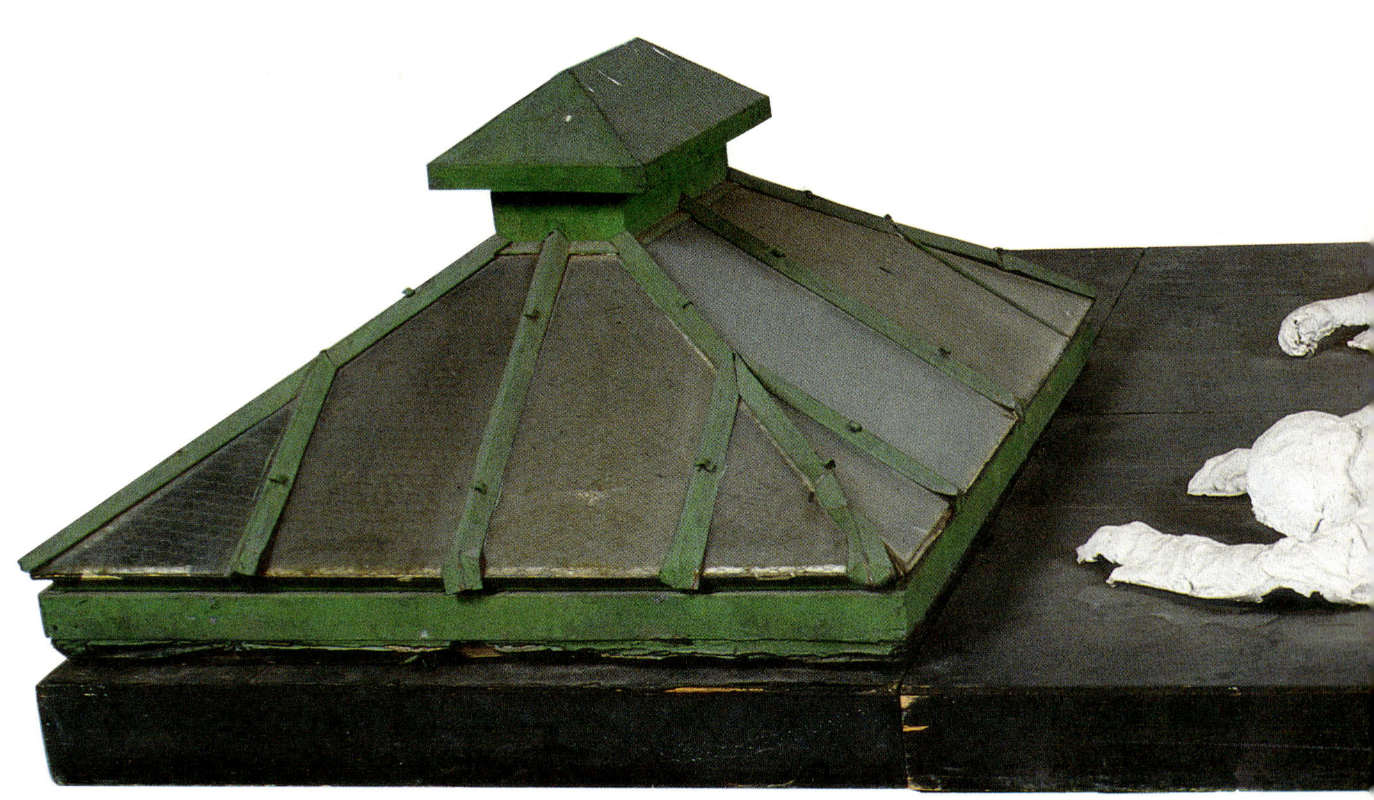

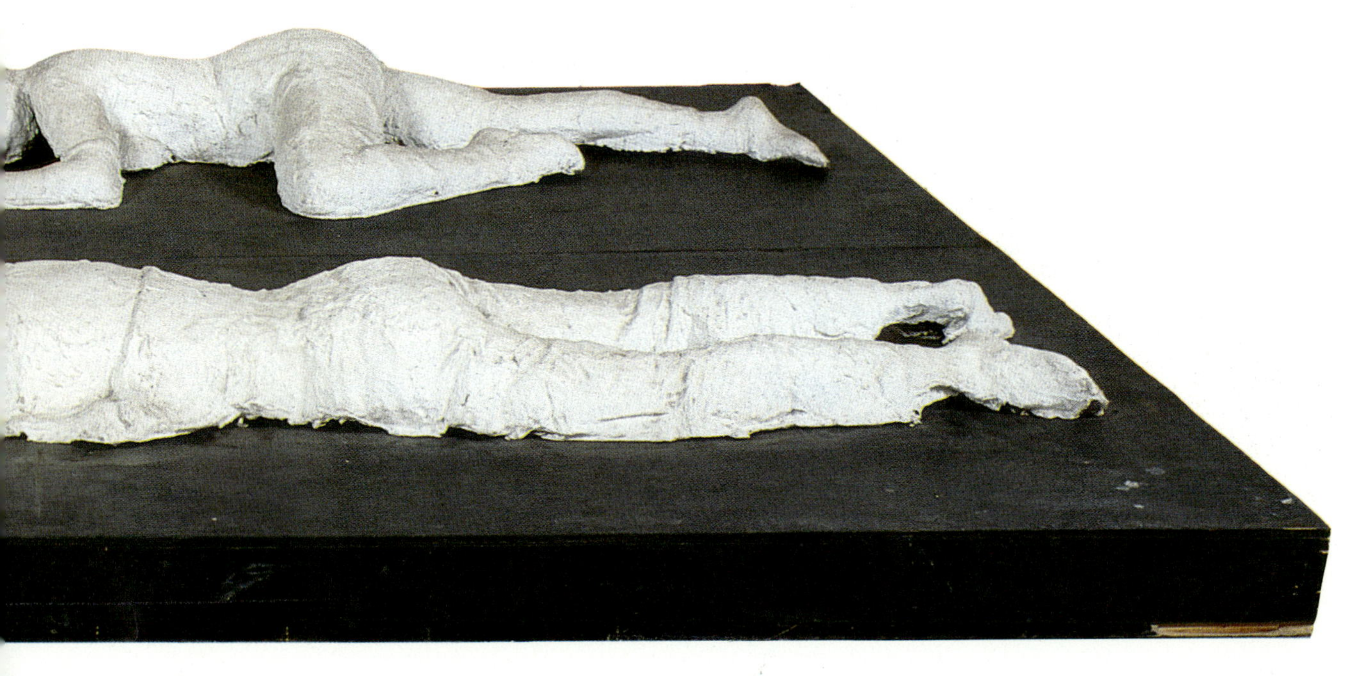

ANTONI TÀPIES

**Grey Relief Perforated by a Black Sign,** 1955
*Mixed media on canvas,*
*57½ x 38¼ in.*

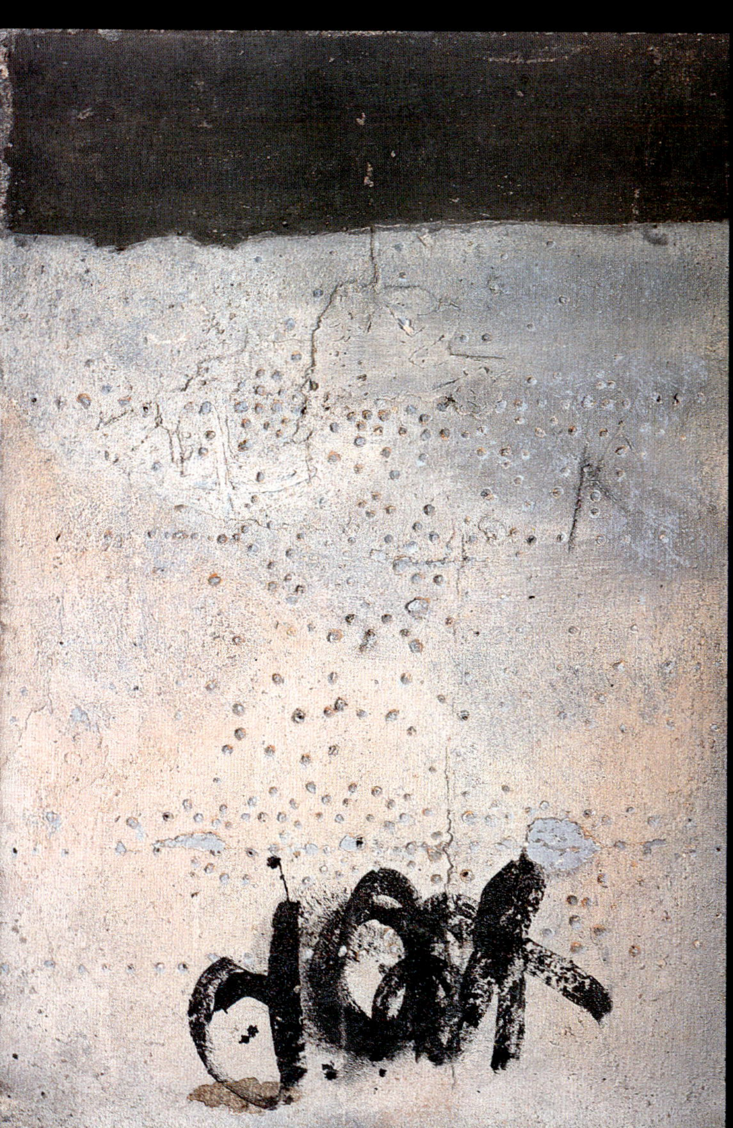

*Mixed media on canvas,*
*76¾ x 51 in.*

**Hammered Grey,** 1959
*Mixed media on canvas,*
*45½ x 35 in.*

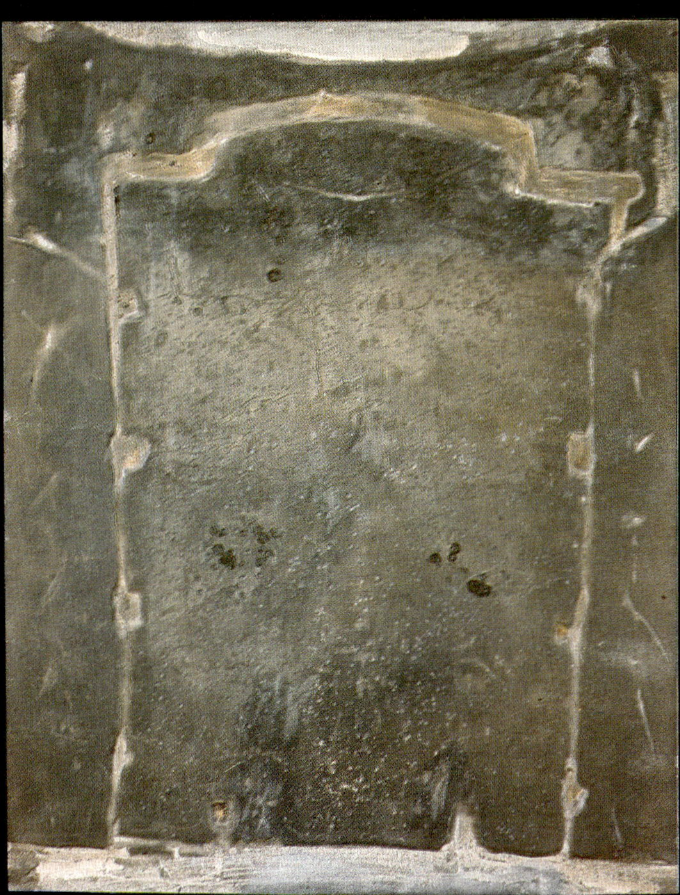

# The Museum of Contemporary Art: The Panza Collection
# Catalogue

**JEAN FAUTRIER**

**Head of a Hostage, No. 1,** 1943
*Oil on paper, 14 x 10½ in.*

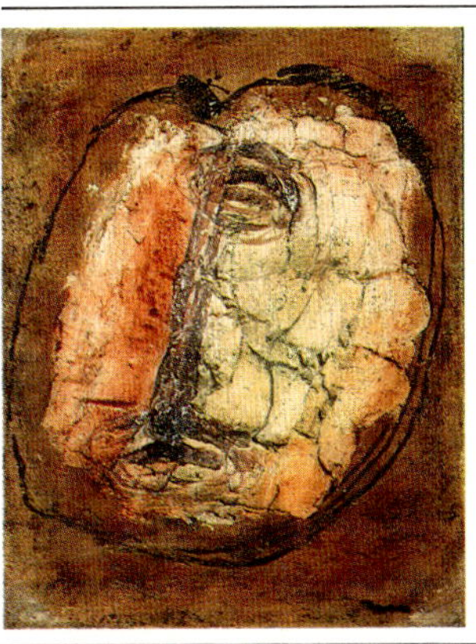

**Nude,** 1943
*Oil on paper, 21½ x 15 in.*

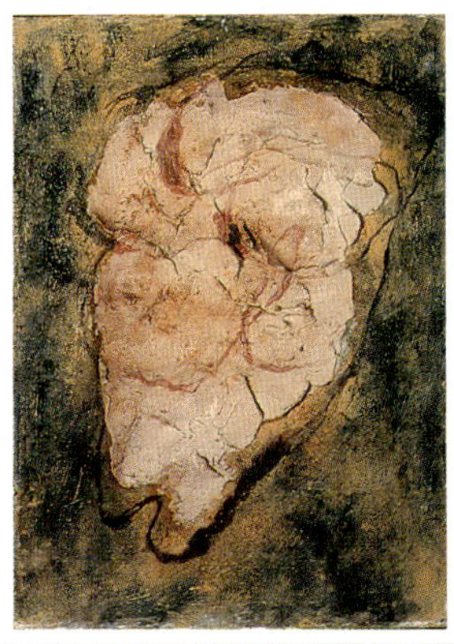

**Head of a Hostage, No. 14,** 1944
*Oil on paper, 13¾ x 10½ in.*

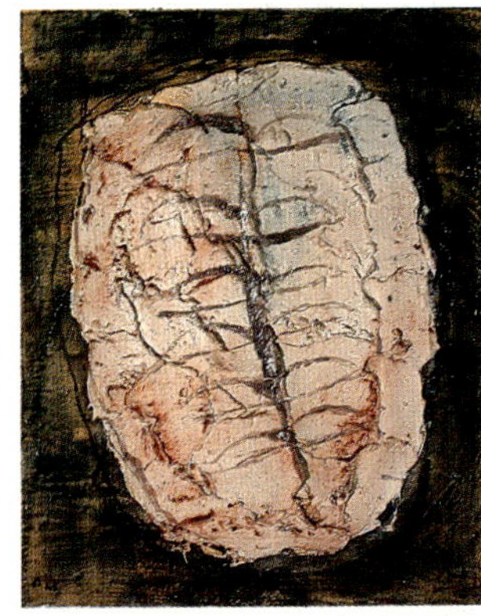

**FRANZ KLINE**

**Tower,** 1953
*Oil on canvas, 81 x 52 in.*

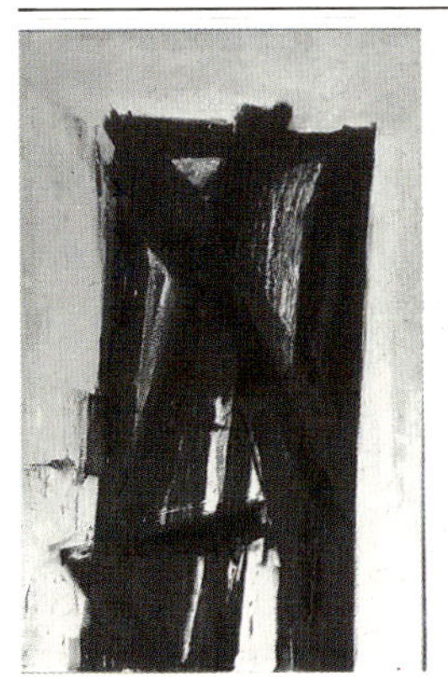

**Thorpe,** 1954
*Oil on canvas, 62 x 43¼ in.*

**Ilza,** 1955
*Oil on canvas, 41¼ x 33 in.*

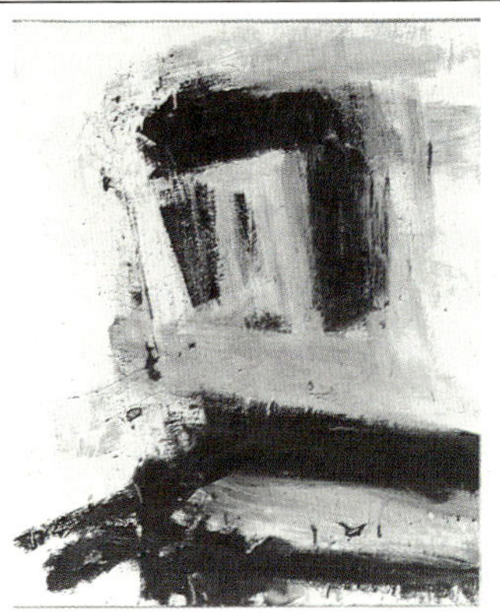

**Alva,** 1958
*Oil on canvas, 40½ x 36½ in.*

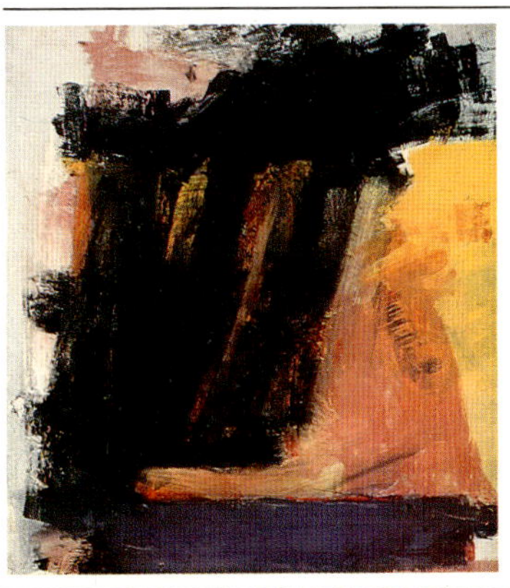

**Line Through White Oblong,** 1959
*Oil on canvas, 60¼ x 81 in.*

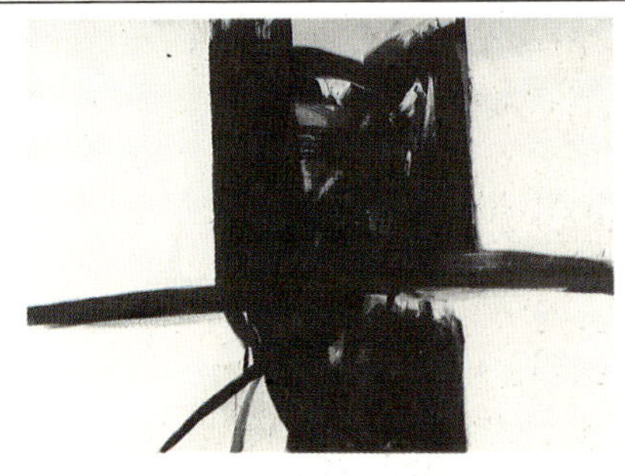

**Orleans,** 1959
*Oil on canvas, 101 x 76 in.*

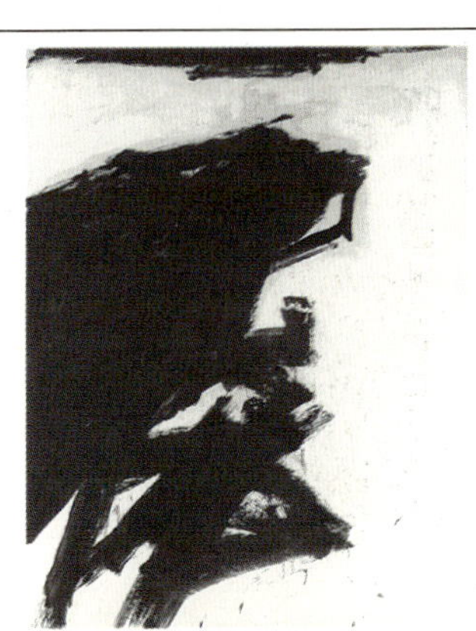

**Profile,** 1945
*Oil on paper, 10½ x 8¼ in.*

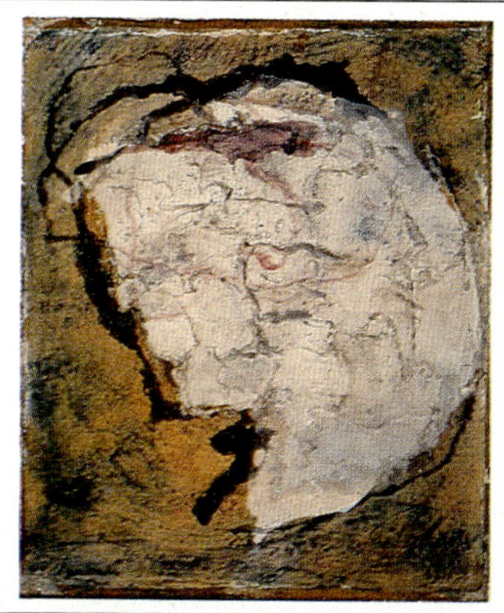

**Remains,** 1946
*Oil on paper, 37¾ x 57½ in.*

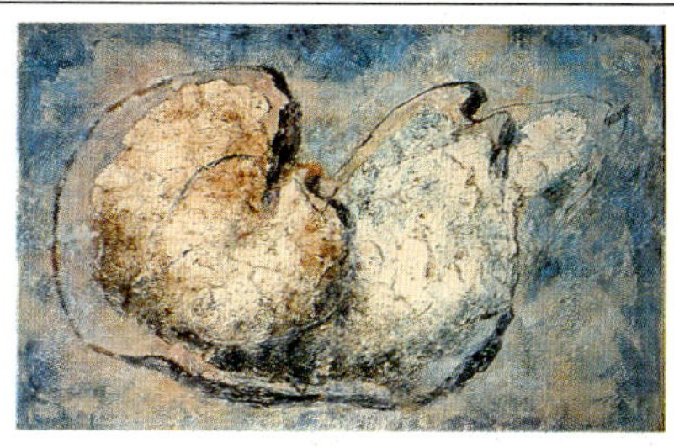

**The Pot,** 1947
*Oil on paper, 13½ x 16 in.*

**Buttress,** 1956
*Oil on canvas, 46½ x 55½ in.*

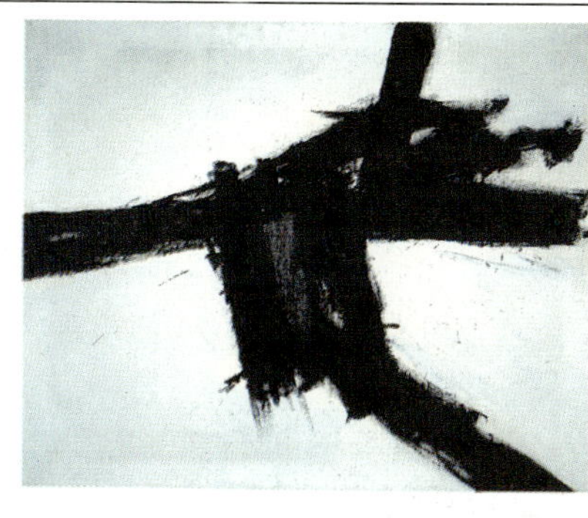

**Monitor,** 1956
*Oil on canvas, 78¾ x 115¾ in.*

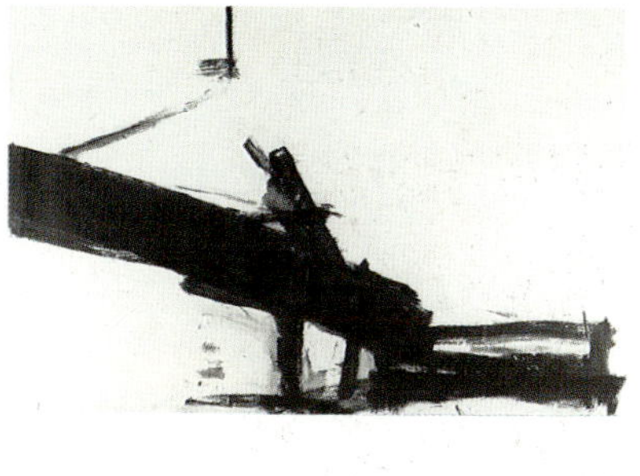

**Black and White,** 1957
*Oil on canvas, 32 x 24 in.*

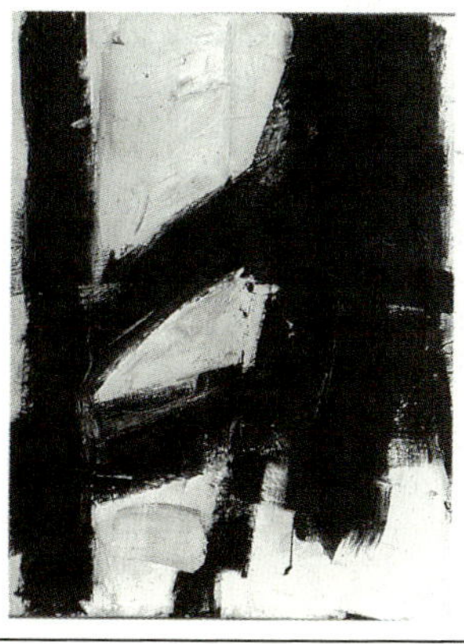

**Hazelton,** 1957
*Oil on canvas, 41¼ x 78 in.*

**Sabro II,** 1959-60
*Oil on canvas, 62 x 79 in.*

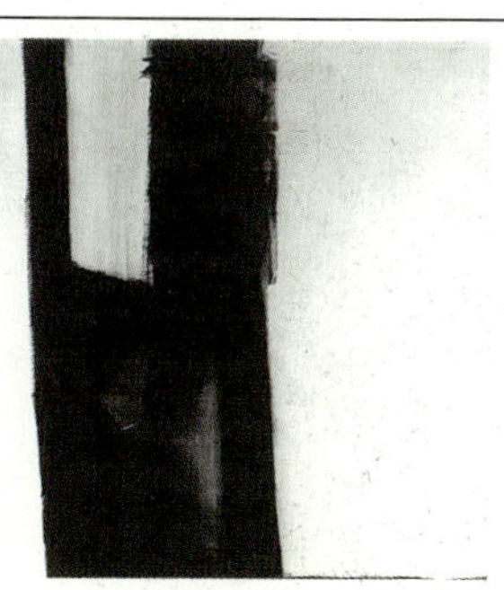

**Black Iris,** 1961
*Oil on canvas, 108¼ x 79½ in.*

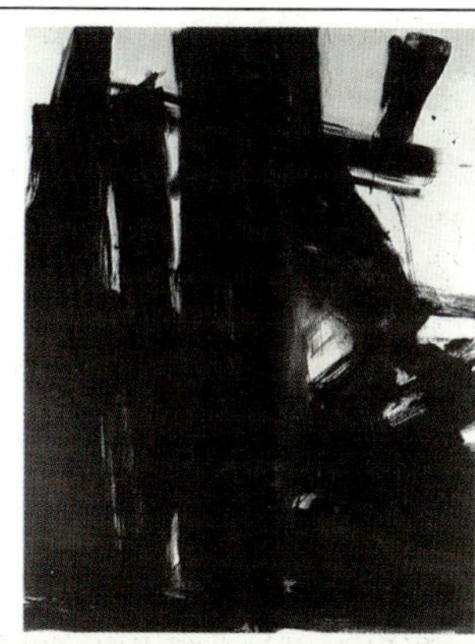

**ROY LICHTENSTEIN**

**Cézanne,** 1962
*Acrylic on canvas, 70 x 48½ in.*

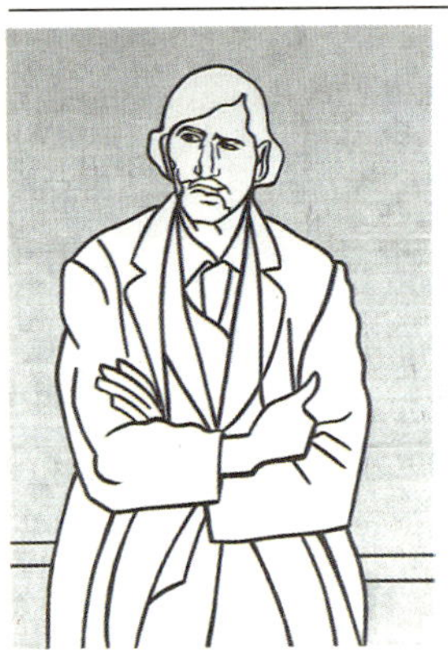

**Desk Calendar,** 1962
*Acrylic on canvas, 48½ x 68 in.*

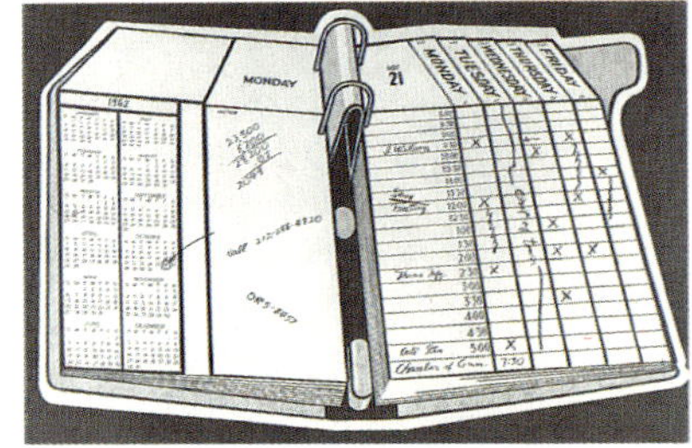

**Meat,** 1962
*Acrylic on canvas, 21¼ x 25¼ in.*

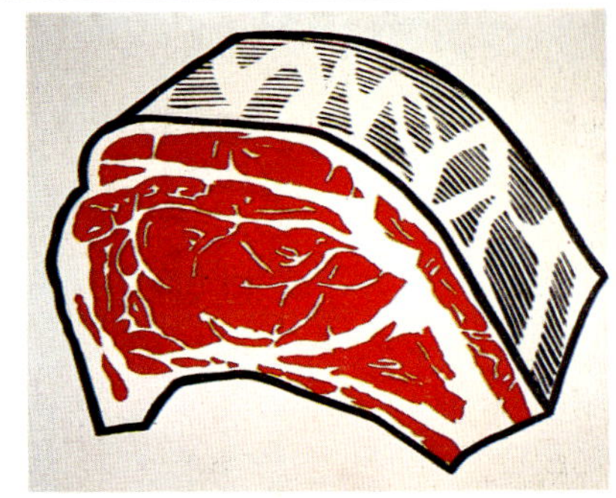

**CLAES OLDENBURG**

**A Brown Shoe,** 1961
*Plaster-soaked muslin over wire frame, painted with enamel, 23½ x 43¼ in.*

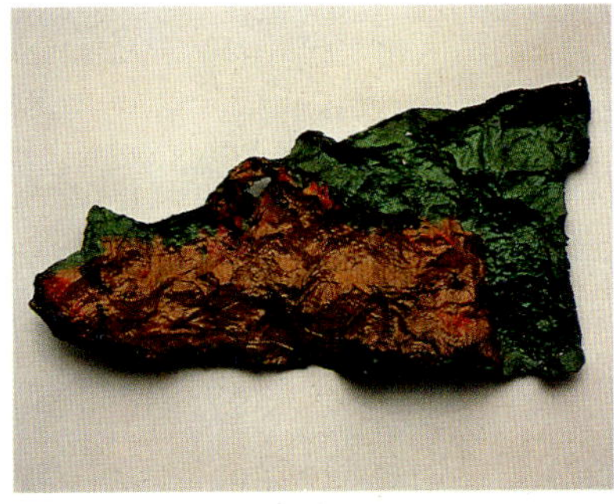

**Blue and Pink Panties,** 1961
*Plaster-soaked muslin over wire frame, painted with enamel, 62¼ x 34¾ x 6 in.*

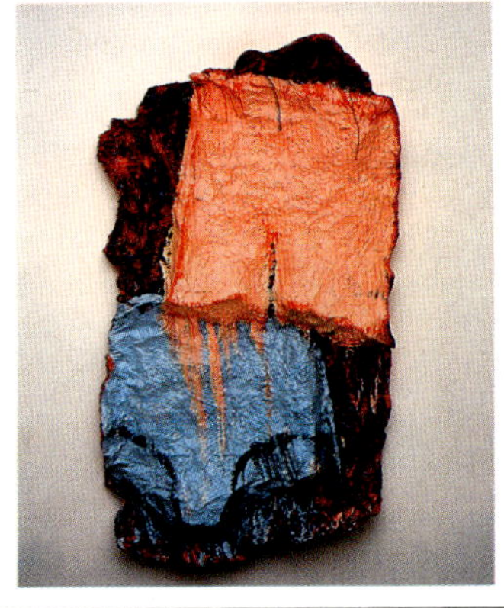

**Bride,** 1961
*Plaster-soaked muslin over wire frame, painted with enamel, 61 x 37½ x 35½ in.*

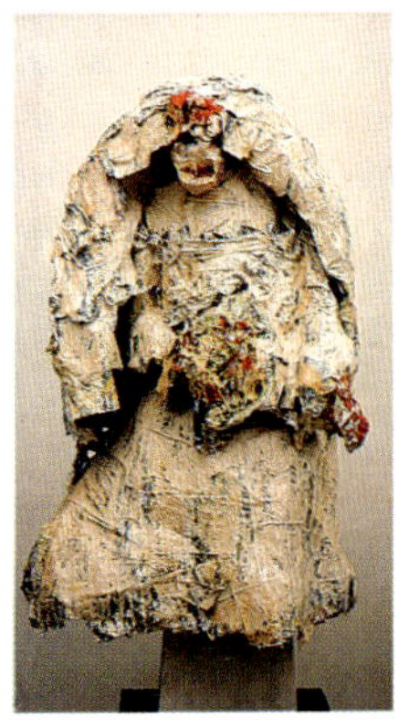

**Pentecostal Cross,** 1961
*Plaster-soaked muslin over wire frame, painted with enamel, 52¾ x 40½ x 6 in.*

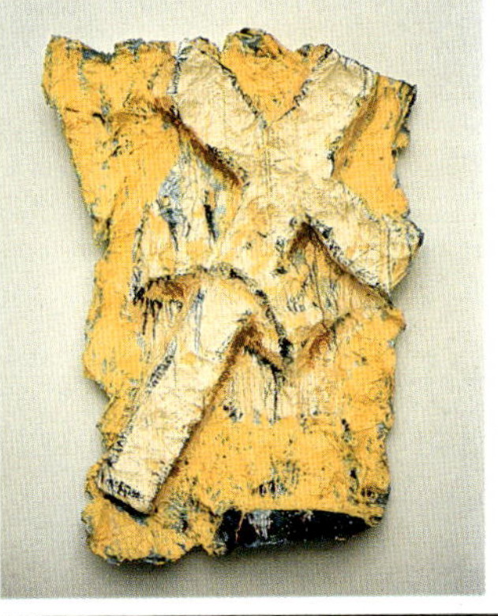

**Pepsi-Cola,** 1961
*Plaster-soaked muslin over wire frame, painted with enamel, 58¼ x 46½ x 7½ in.*

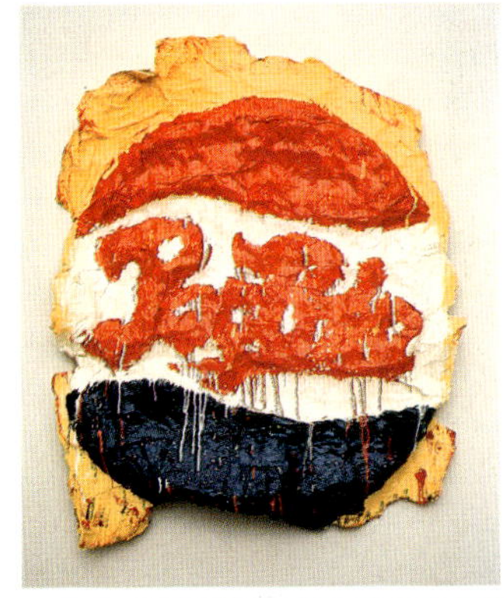

**Blue Pants on Chair,** 1962
*Plaster-soaked muslin over wire frame, painted with enamel, 37 x 17 x 26¾ in.*

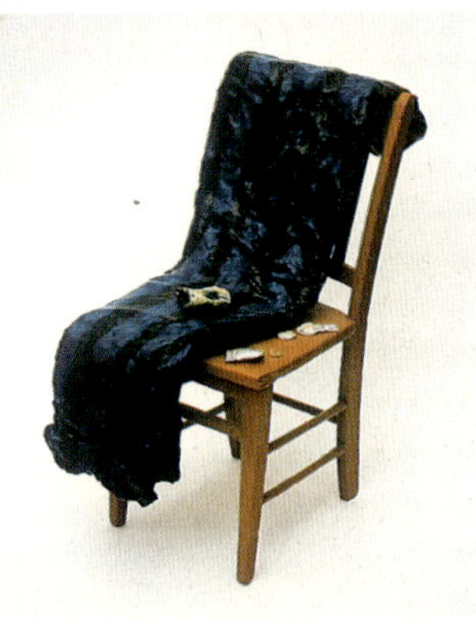

**Strong Hand (The Grip),** 1962
*Acrylic on canvas, 30 x 30¼ in.*

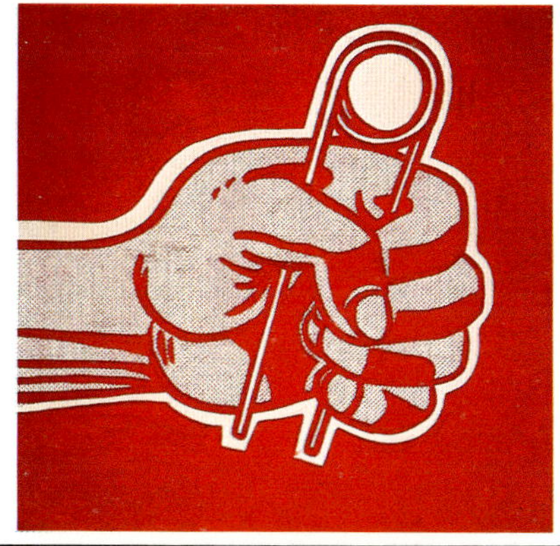

**Cigarette Fragment,** 1961
*Plaster-soaked muslin over wire frame, painted with enamel, 32¾ x 30¾ x 6¾ in.*

**Fragment of Candy in a Box,** 1961
*Plaster-soaked muslin over wire frame, painted with enamel, 44 x 32 x 6 in.*

**Green Stocking,** 1961
*Plaster-soaked muslin over wire frame, painted with enamel, 43¼ x 18 in.*

**Mu Mu,** 1961
*Plaster-soaked muslin over wire frame, painted with enamel, 63½ x 41¼ x 4 in.*

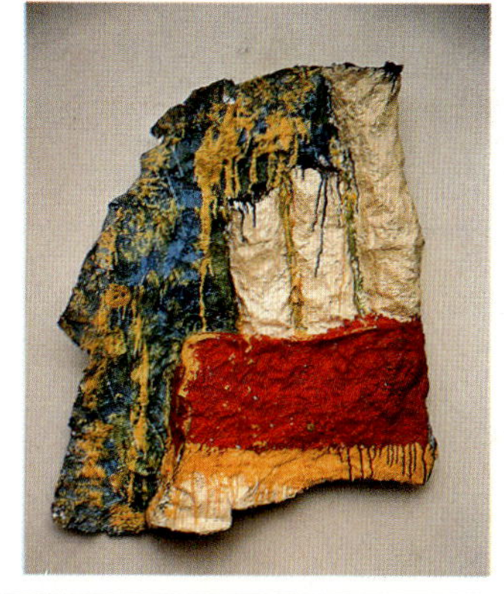

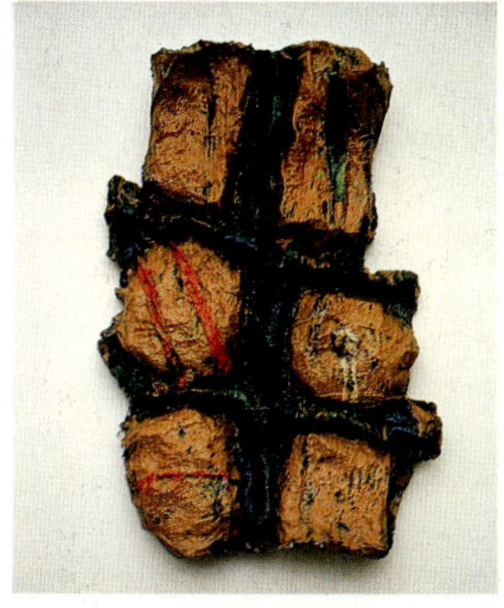

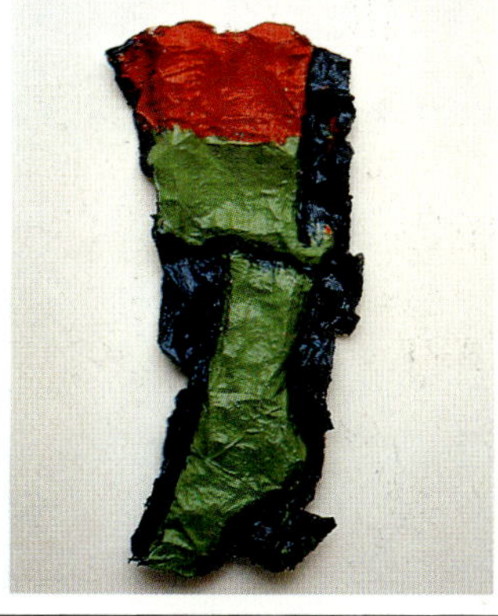

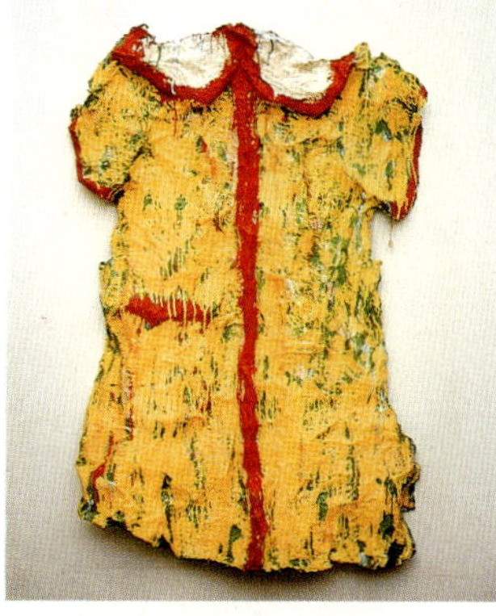

**Breakfast Table,** 1962
*Plaster-soaked muslin over wire frame, painted with enamel, 34½ x 35½ x 34½ in.*

**Hamburger,** 1962
*Plaster-soaked muslin over wire frame, painted with enamel, 7 x 9 x 9 in.*

**Pie à la Mode,** 1962
*Plaster-soaked muslin over wire frame, painted with enamel, 22 x 18½ x 11¾ in.*

**Tennis Shoes,** 1962
*Plaster-soaked muslin over wire frame, painted with enamel, 24 x 24 x 10 in.*

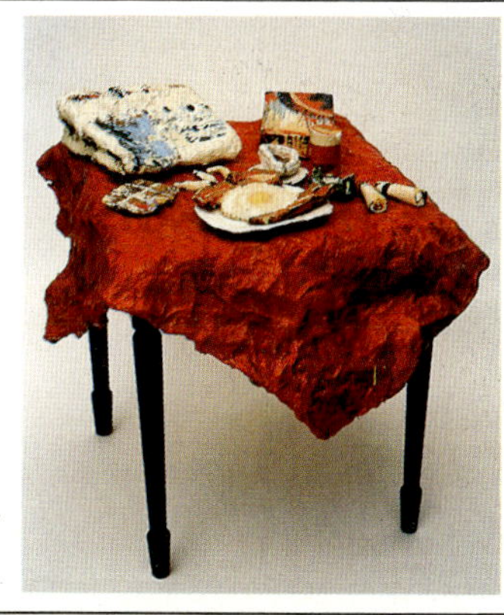

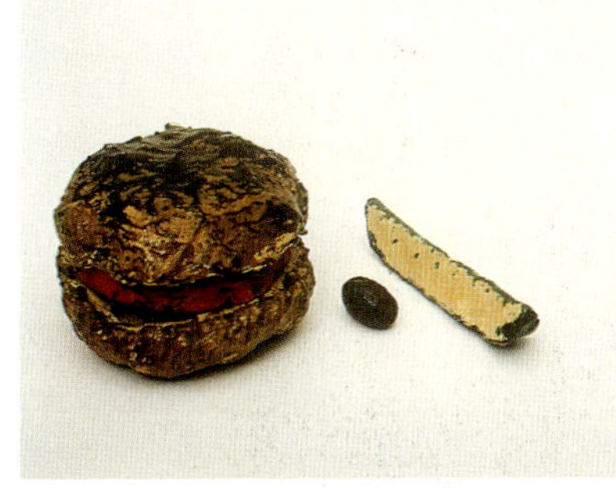

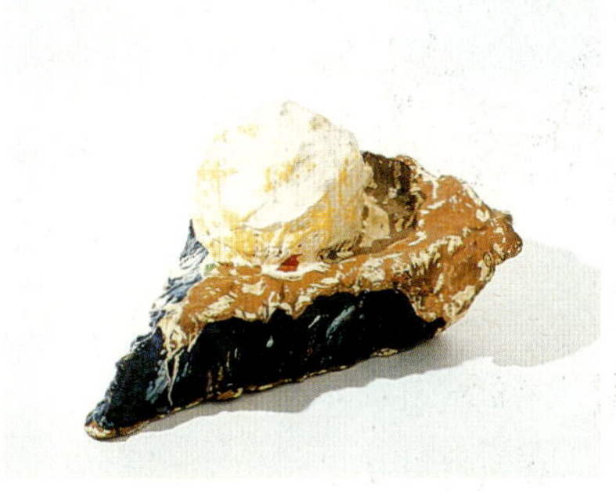

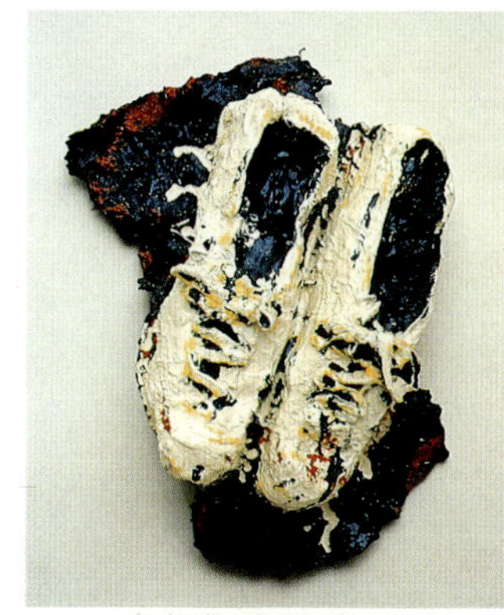

**Umbrella and Newspaper,** 1962
*Plaster-soaked muslin over wire frame, painted with enamel, 38½ x 19½ x 6 in.*

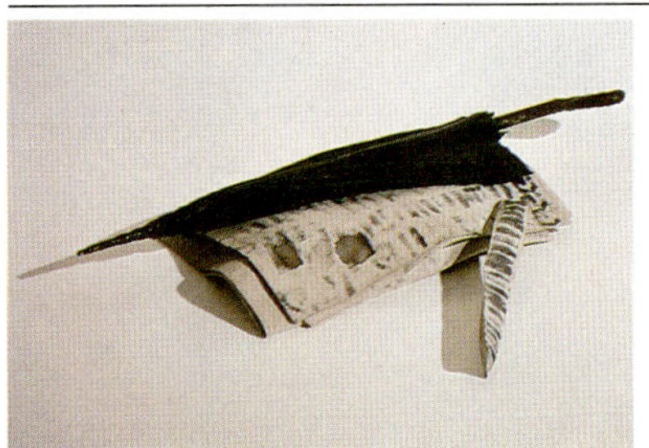

**White Shirt on Chair,** 1962
*Plaster-soaked muslin over wire frame, painted with enamel, 39¾ x 30 x 25¼ in.*

## ROBERT RAUSCHENBERG

**Interview,** 1955
*Combine painting, 72¾ x 49¼ in.*

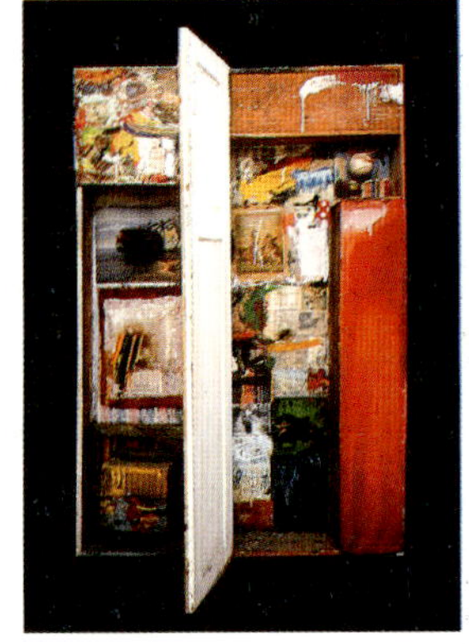

**Untitled Combine,** 1955
*Combine painting, 86½ x 37 x 26¼ in.*

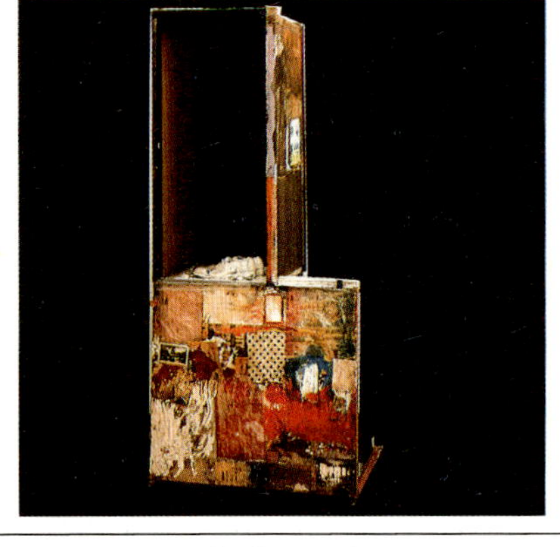

**Small Rebus,** 1956
*Combine painting, 35 x 46 in.*

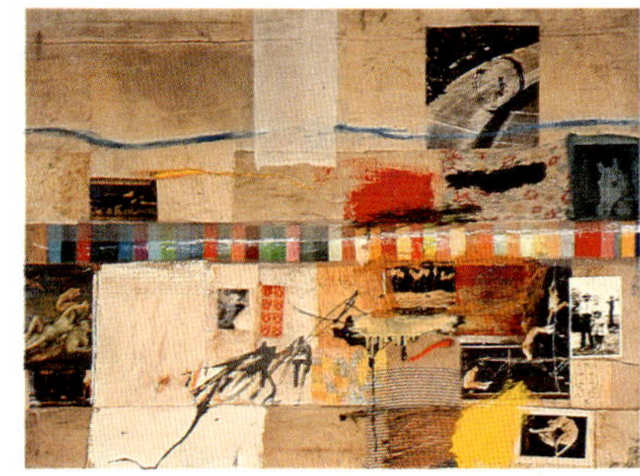

**Kickback,** 1959
*Combine painting, 75 x 32 in.*

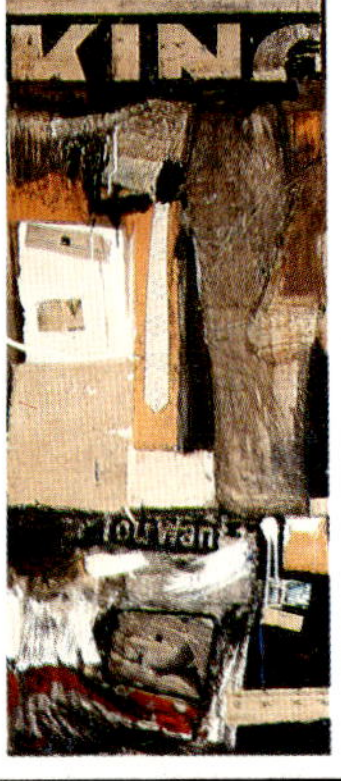


**Painting with Grey Wing,** 1959
*Combine painting, 31 x 21 in.*

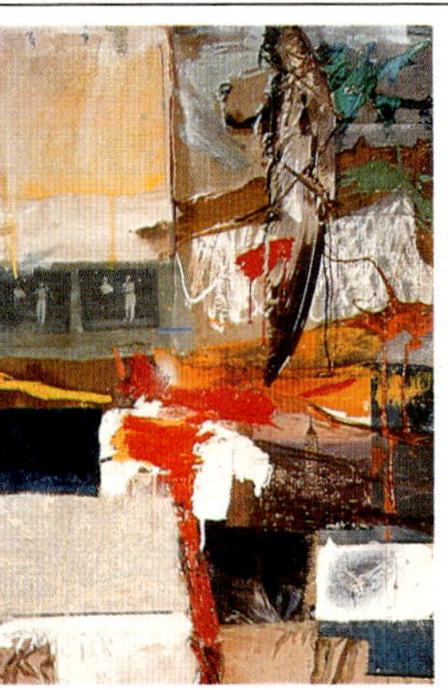

**South Carolina Fall,** 1961
*Combine painting, 55 x 20 in.*

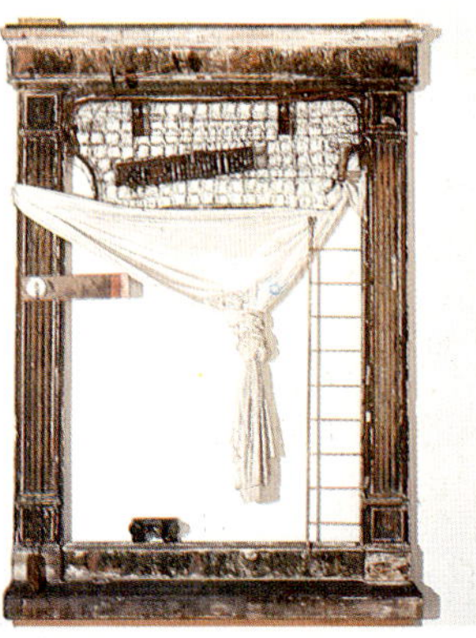

**Factum I,** 1957
*Combine painting, 61½ x 35¾ in.*

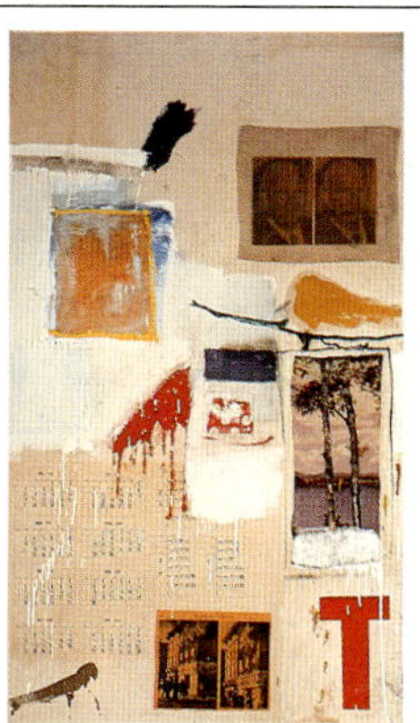

**Coca-Cola Plan,** 1958
*Combine painting, 26¾ x 25¼ x 4¾ in.*

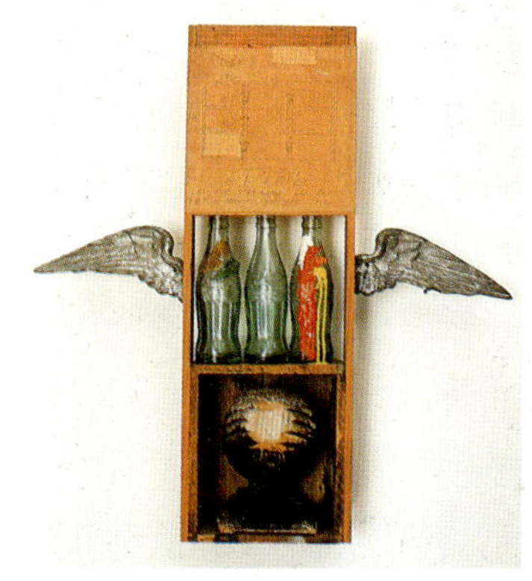

**Gift for Apollo,** 1959
*Combine painting, 43¾ x 29½ in.*

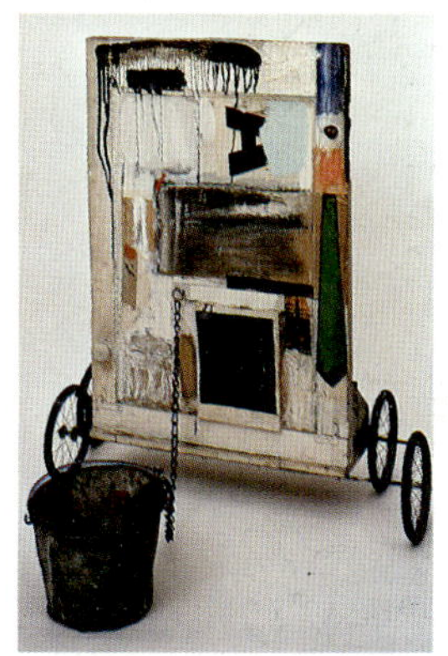

**Inlet,** 1959
*Combine painting, 84½ x 48½ in.*

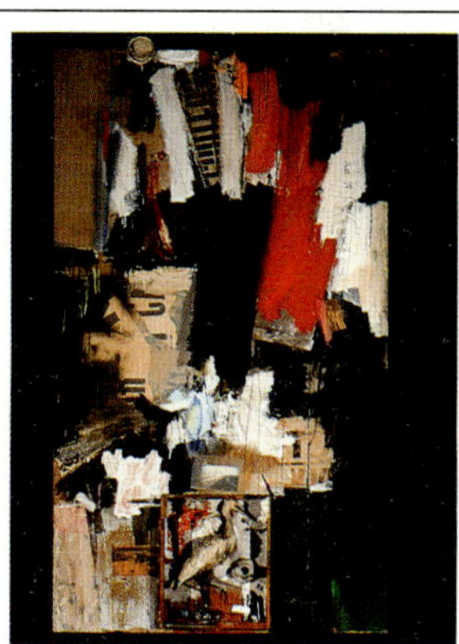

**Trophy III,** 1961
*Combine painting, 96 x 65¾ in.*

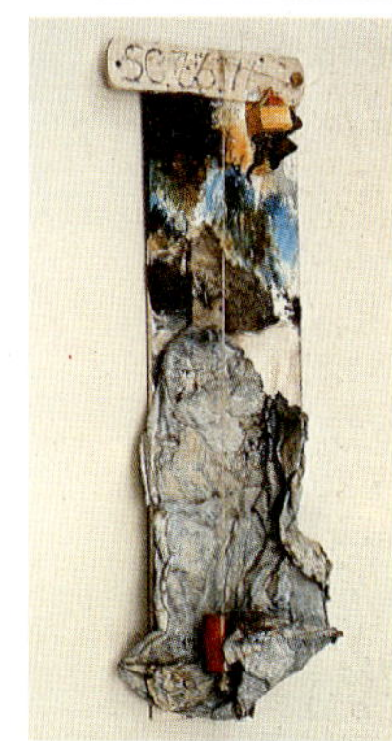

**JAMES ROSENQUIST**

**Push Button,** 1960-61
*Oil on canvas, 82¾ x 105½ in.*

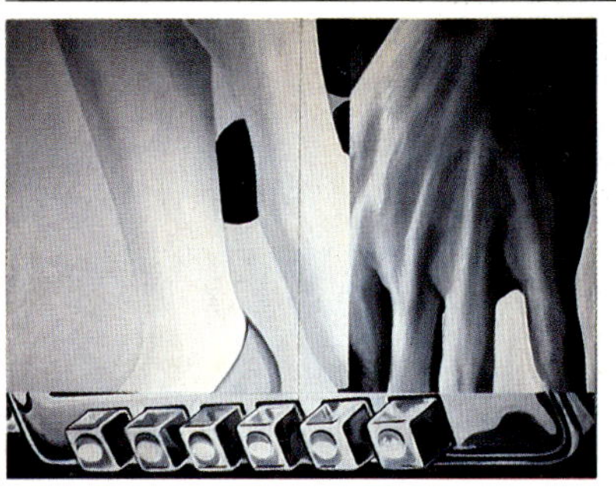

**White Cigarette,** 1961
*Oil on canvas, 60½ x 35¾ in.*

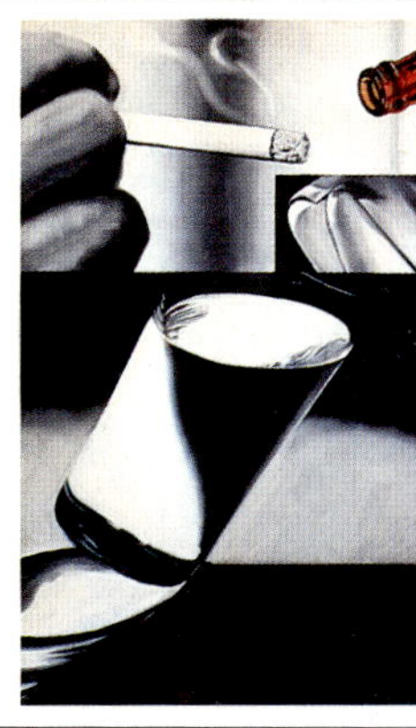

**A Lot to Like,** 1962
*Oil on canvas, 92½ x 203 in.*

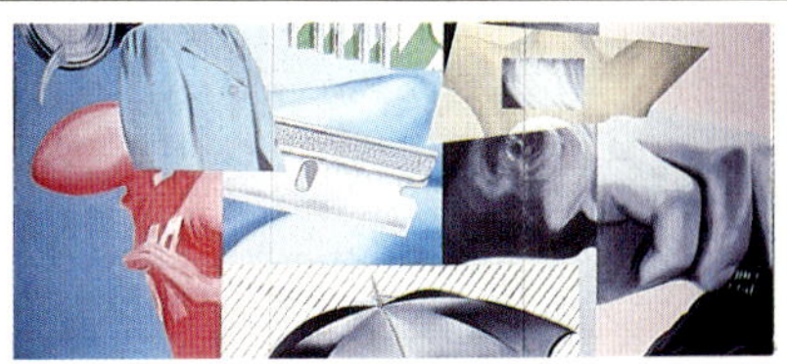

**Shave,** 1964
*Oil on canvas, 58¼ x 50½ in.*

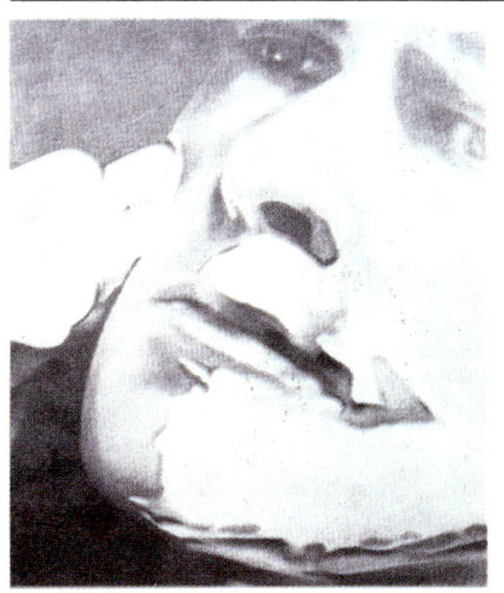

**MARK ROTHKO**

**Brown, Blue, Brown on Blue,** 1953
*Oil on canvas, 115¾ x 91¼ in.*

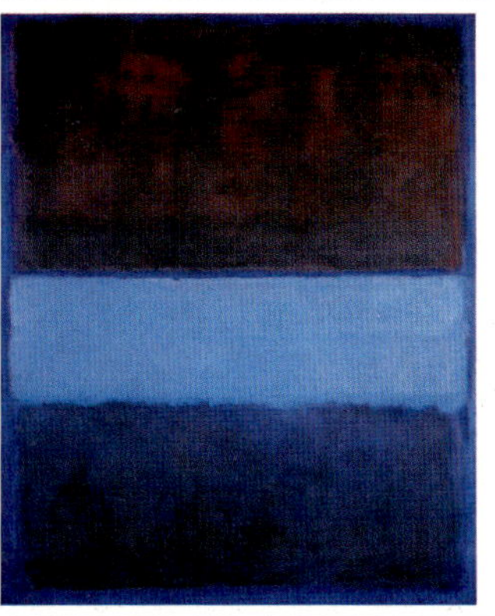

**Violet and Yellow on Rose,** 1954
*Oil on canvas, 83½ x 67¾ in.*

**Black, Ochre, Red Over Red,** 1957
*Oil on canvas, 99¼ x 81½ in.*

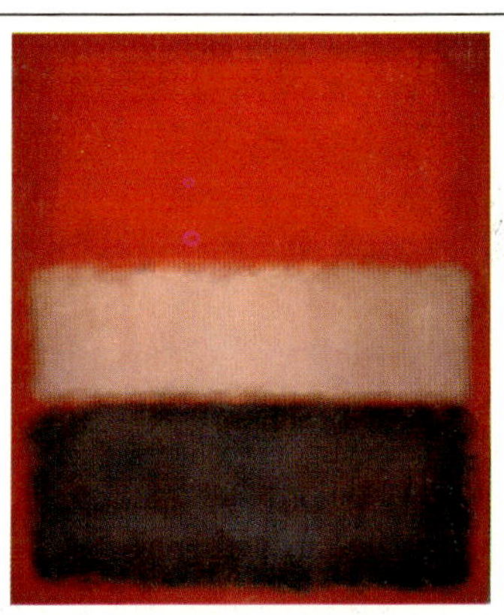

**Capillary Action,** 1962
*Oil on canvas, 92½ x 136¼ in.*

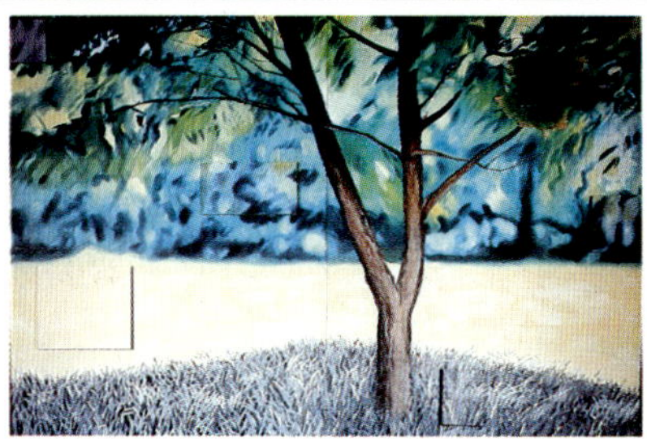

**Noon,** 1962
*Oil on canvas, 36¼ x 48½ in.*

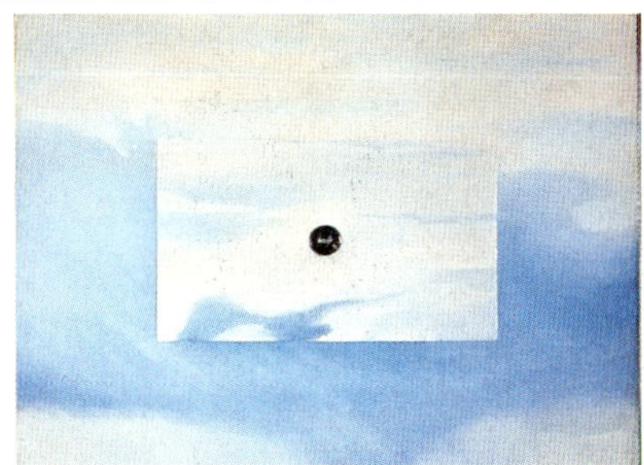

**Vestigal Appendage,** 1962
*Oil on canvas, 72 x 93¼ in.*

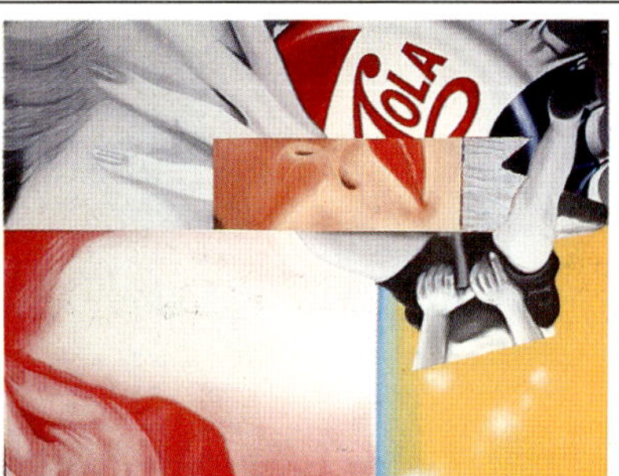

**Waves,** 1962
*Oil on canvas, 56 x 77 in.*

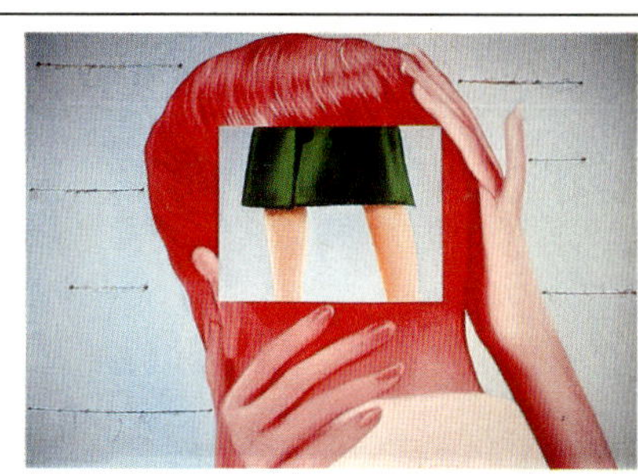

**Purple Brown,** 1957
*Oil on canvas, 84 x 72 in.*

**Red and Brown,** 1957
*Oil on canvas, 68 x 43 in.*

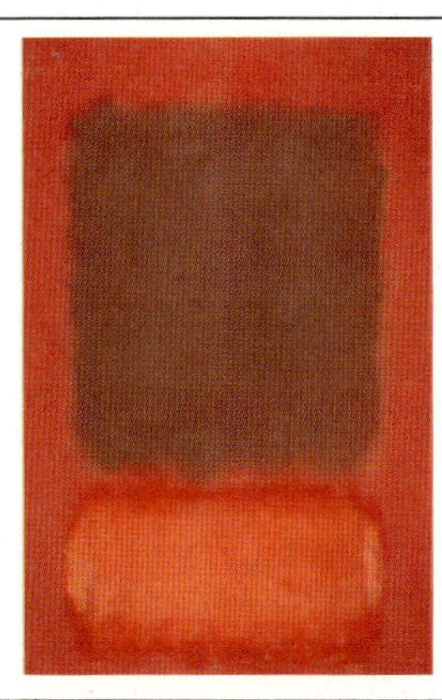

**Red and Blue Over Red,** 1959
*Oil on canvas, 93 x 80¾ in.*

**Black on Dark Sienna on Purple,** 1960
*Oil on canvas, 119¼ x 105 in.*

## GEORGE SEGAL

**Sunbathers on Rooftop,** 1963-67
*Plaster and wood,*
*34¼ x 143½ x 96 in.*

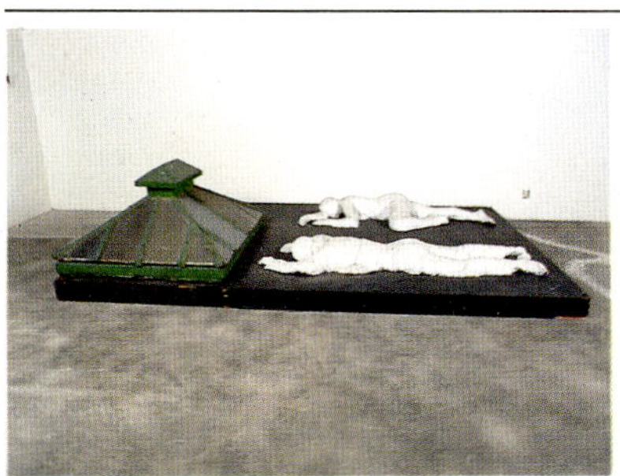

**Man in the Armchair,** 1969
*Plaster and wood,*
*49½ x 30 x 31½ in.*

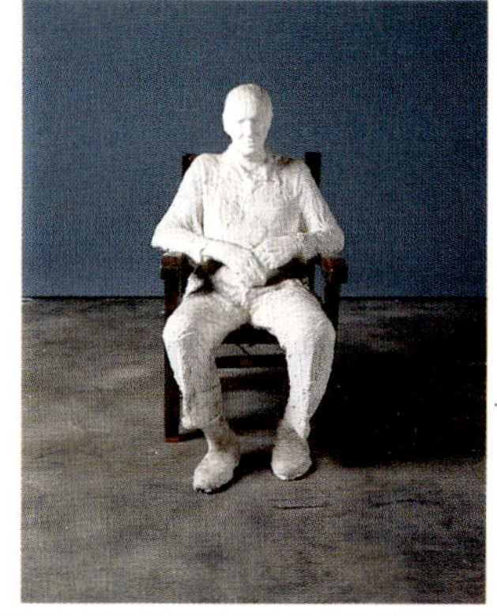

## ANTONI TÀPIES

**All White,** 1955
*Mixed media on canvas,*
*57½ x 38¼ in.*

**Grey and Black Cross,** 1955
*Mixed media on canvas,*
*57½ x 45 in.*

**Grey Relief Perforated by a Black Sign,** 1955
*Mixed media on canvas,*
*57½ x 38¼ in.*

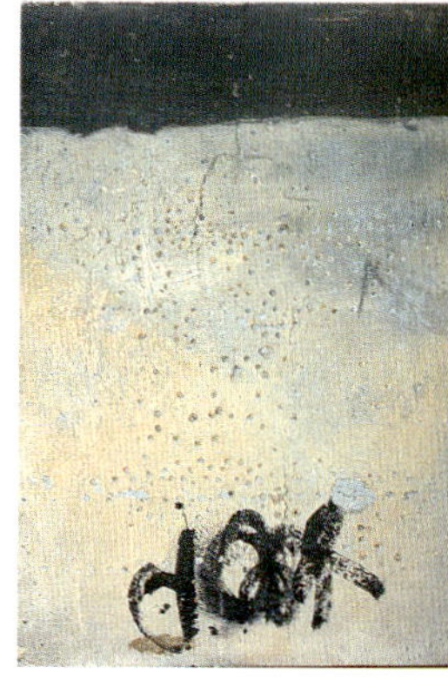

**Ochre and Brown—New York,** 1957
*Mixed media on canvas,*
*21¼ x 32 in.*

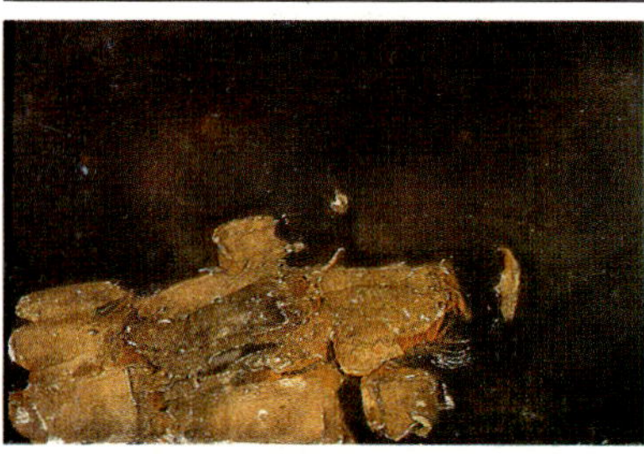

**Perforated Body,** 1957
*Mixed media on canvas,*
*57½ x 45 in.*

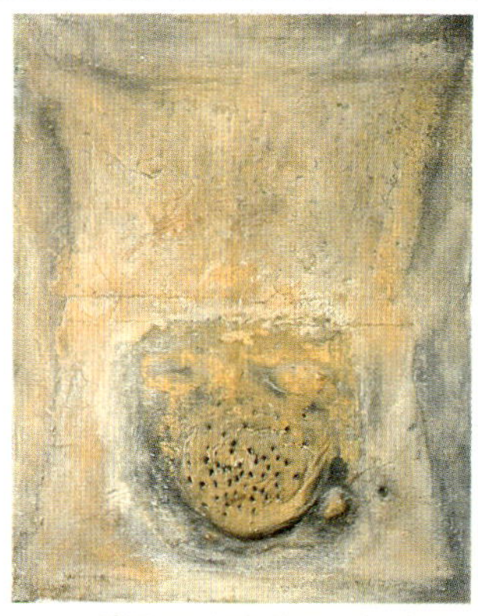

**Sable Ochre,** 1957
*Mixed media on canvas,*
*76¾ x 51 in.*

**Collage on a Black Ground; Hommage to Gaudi,** 1956
*Mixed media on canvas,*
*51¼ x 63¾ in.*

**Grey on White,** 1956
*Mixed media on canvas,*
*51¼ x 63¾ in.*

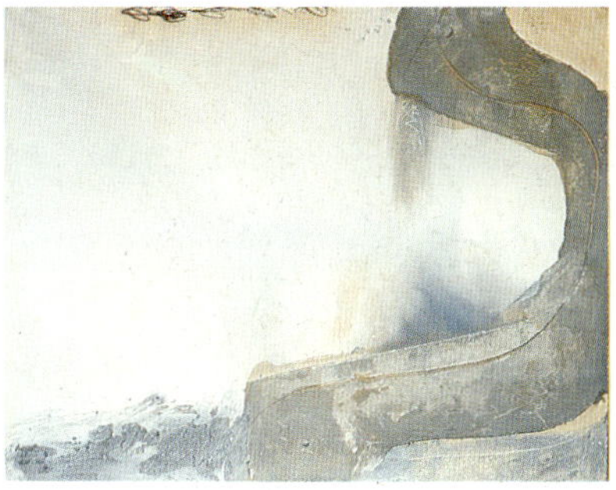

**Brown-Ochre with Black Crevice,** 1957
*Mixed media on canvas,*
*51¼ x 38¼ in.*

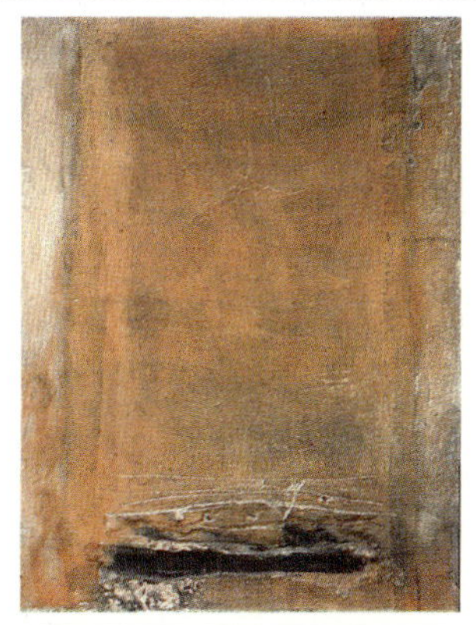

**Grey-Brown Composition,** 1957
*Mixed media on canvas,*
*35 x 51 in.*

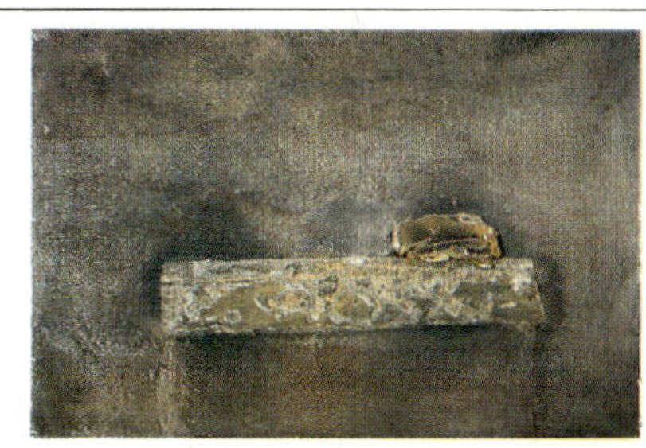

**Grey with Red Sign,** 1958
*Mixed media on canvas,*
*57½ x 35 in.*

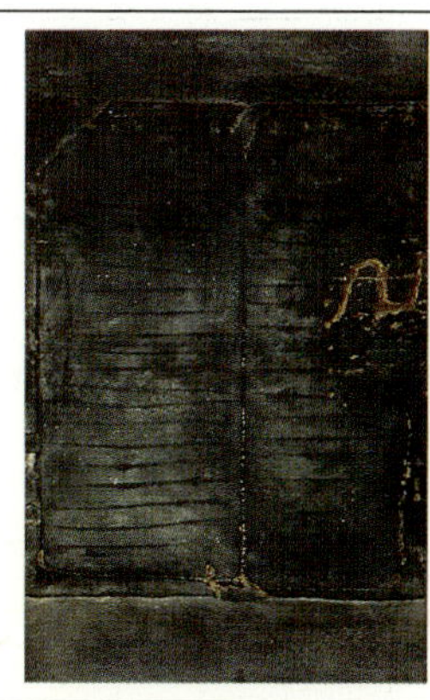

**Red-Brown,** 1958
*Mixed media on canvas,*
*45 x 57½ in.*

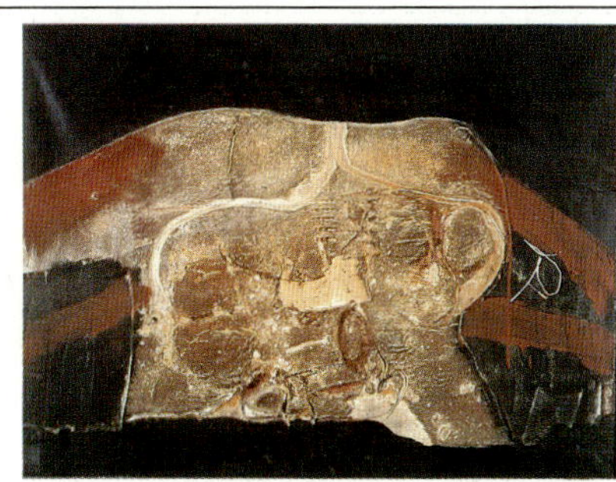

**Brown-Grey with Six Marks,** 1959
*Mixed media on canvas,*
*102¼ x 74¾ in.*

**Hammered Grey,** 1959
*Mixed media on canvas,*
*45½ x 35 in.*

**Staff**

John Bowsher, *Operations Manager*
Kim Bradley, *Registrar*
Kerry Brougher, *Assistant Curator*
Julia Brown, *Senior Curator*
Lessie Brown, *Receptionist*
Connie Butler, *Curatorial Intern*
Jacqueline Crist, *Assistant Curator*
Natasha Ebeling-Koning, *Registrarial Assistant*
Nancy Fleeter, *Controller*
Sherri Geldin, *Administrator*
Ann Goldstein, *Grant Writer*
Robin Hanson, *Development Assistant*
Sylvia Hohri, *Public Outreach Coordinator*
Sue Johnson, *Director of Membership*
June Kino-Cullen, *Curatorial Secretary*
Richard Koshalek, *Director*
Cardie Kremer, *Development Assistant*
Julie Lazar, *Curator*
Julie Mayerson, *Office/Personnel Manager*
Patricia Needham, *Campaign Director*
Patty Paine, *Curatorial Secretary*
Jill Quinn, *Campaign Secretary*
Nancy Rogers, *Administrative Assistant*
Alma Ruiz, *Executive Assistant*
John Seed, *Bookstore Manager*
Deborah Seid, *Curatorial Secretary*
Elizabeth Smith, *Assistant Curator*
Pamela Wilson, *Campaign Assistant*
Polly Wilson, *Assistant Bookkeeper*
Rhyan Zweifler, *Membership Secretary*

**Board of Trustees**